BUSHI KARATE

CW00591636

"Advanced Basics, The Science

By

K O'Connor (Dip Sports Psychology)

(7th dan karate jitsu, 7th dan karate do, 6th dan jujitsu, 1st dan Aikido)

K.B.I. Overseas Instructor & deputy examiner 1982 – 8
Assistant coach, police study group 1983 – 89
I.M.A.F. Technical Director for Karate (GB) 1989 – 90
B.K.J.J.A member of technical standards committee 1991 – 93
B.J.J.A. Jujitsu Instructor (level 1) 1993 – 94
B.K.J.J.A. Regional executive officer 1994
B.K.J.A. Founder and Chairman 1999
Shorin jujitsu (Kuwait). Kancho/ Founder 2002

My thanks to all the Instructors I have worked and studied with around the world over the past thirty years. For the dedication, skill and knowledge they shared and for the standards they set and passed on to me.
A special thanks goes out to my friend Denis King, without whom this book would not have been published.
Also my wife Dawn who has supported me as a friend and assisted me as a Yudansha seven days a week during classes, seminars and courses both here and abroad.

First published in Great Britain by BKJA Promotions 2002

All text and drawings copyright Kevin O'Connor 2002

Cover Photograph by M J S Photographic & Video Services

Kevin O'Connor asserts the moral right to be identified as the author of this work

The copyright on all illustrations is owned by Kevin O'Connor

Produced in Great Britain by
Cande
Park Hall Works
Sutherland Road
Longton
Stoke-on-Trent

British Library Cataloguing-in-Publication Data
A catalogue record for this book is available from the British Library

ISBN 0 9544223 0 9

Preface

My learning began within an Association, which taught all aspects of Japanese martial arts. From karate, judo, aikido and kendo, into the specialist in depth forms of Naganata do and Kyudo. Although I have not trained in depth, in some of these forms, I learned much from observation and discussion with the various Sensei. It is from their knowledge that my understanding developed with a fullness and awareness of the true technique. Rigid karate became a flowing form of cutting and penetrating blocks combined with true striking potential. An open mindedness, which allowed me to strike with a block, and block with a strike.

The stances and stepping developed from the integration of karate and aikido ideals. Combining balance and posture, whilst control and fluidity grew from the kendo and the jo staff practice. This emphasising that we do not defend ourselves in stances but pass through them in the course of completing a defensive manoeuvre. A positive stance being completed at the Kime (focus point) of the movement. In this way, not committing oneself to a fighting posture, you can move with your opponent in a natural way, instead of an opposing way. Thus enabling you to turn your opponent's force back upon himself. In this way we achieve the understanding "Karate ni sente nashi" (There is no first strike in Karate).

Fundamental

Through my teachers and methods of practice I understand the old principals that basics and kata are everything. They provide all the training to improve technique and all the mental vision and stimulation to improve posture, mental awareness and focus, co-ordinating mind and body towards the goal of becoming one with your opponent. Focus of mind, speed of reflexes, movement and posture of the body are the stages, from your opponents strike to your immediate counter providing a full circle of events in the shortest possible time and minimum amount of effort.

Photo taken of the author in 1974,
Having just obtained shodan from the "Cho to Ken Budo Renmei". An organisation that would introduced him to great masters like Abbe, Segino, Mochizuki, Tachibana, Sato and others over the next 10 years

Basics

The basics are the same techniques of all the major styles i.e. lunge punch (oi tsuki), front kick (mae geri), low level block (gedan - barai), bent wrist lock (kote ku can setsu), which are practiced by all martial artists. It is the mind and the attitude of the student, whilst delivering these techniques, which creates the effect, the result, and even the very basis of a style or school. All to often a student is taught that a certain technique must be a punch and another technique should be a block, and so it is that a great amount of feeling (and effect) is lost within that technique. This attitude also restricts the student's mind and prevents him from producing the best effect from his technique.

Many students, when told to punch, punch out with the feeling of smashing something. Tension then overthrows the effectiveness of the body weight and its direction, so reducing the potential of the punch quite drastically. At this stage a student will still put "kime" at the end of a technique, bringing it to a stop, producing a percussion blow or "thump". Eventually, however it will be the middle of the technique, and so pass on through the opponent.

Any block can be a punch and every punch can effectively incorporate a block. It is with this feeling in mind that we shall enter into the basics of technique.

Contents

Stances

We shall begin here, as all movements and techniques either pass through, or focus their energy at the end of a stance.

Zenkutsu Dachi (Front stance)

In shotokan and Shotokai schools emphasis is laid on low postures and a centre of gravity for stability and power. We can step forwards from one stance through into this stance. Application can be made moving forwards from an upright natural position (Hachi dachi). Even stepping backwards from a previous position. However at the moment of focus the hips should always be moving forwards and a feeling downward from "Hara" to maximise the potential of the accompanying block or strike. The hips may be square to the front or angled depending on the block or strike being used. One should have a feeling of sinking the hips forwards and downwards and the feet are approximately shoulder width apart. The back leg being locked, with the foot turned at an angle to the front, enabling a better grip to the floor. The front leg is bent with the knee over the ankle. The hip, knee, ankle and foot in line to the front. When stepping, pull with the front knee, and thrust the hips forward, keeping the body upright. Do not lead with the head and shoulders, this weakens the body posture and pushes the face into the attack. The body weight will be brought onto the front leg, so that at the mid point of the step, the back leg has no weight upon it. The result being that the leg can slide into the forward position easily, followed by the hip weight, so that it is used to add power and mass behind the hand technique. It also means that the back leg could easily be raised at the mid step to change direction,, balance or the final technique (either hand or foot).

When stepping through, keep the feet shoulder width apart and the supporting leg bent. The hips and therefore the whole body travel on a horizontal plane, not up and down in a wave like motion. This is important for both speed and stability. Keep both feet flat on the floor (on smooth surfaces). As the back foot passes the front, turn the front foot outwards at forty five degrees, this will help to keep it flat at the point when maximum weight is over it and it is already in the position for the leg to lock at the rear.

Kokutsu Dachi (Back Stance)

Here the body is thirty to forty five degrees to the front, the heels are on one line and sixty percent of the body weight is over the rear leg. Both feet are at right angles to each other, the front and knee pointing forward with the leg slightly bent. The rear foot points to the side with the knee pushing back over the ankle. This provides stability, combined with a strong defence against attack to the rear leg.

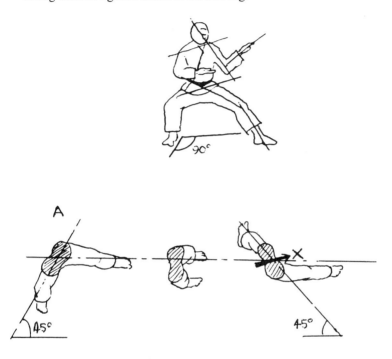

From A. pull with the front knee. Step through bringing the hips square and the knees bent slightly (as B). Slide foot forwards along a centre line and pushing the hip forward to position C. Push the hips forward and down towards point X. For entrance and stability. Keep the hip, knee and foot in line, do not sag the knee inwards as this will weaken the posture and create an opening against the knee for ashi barai (foot sweep).

Maintain push against the back knee with the feeling of kiba dachi (horse stance).

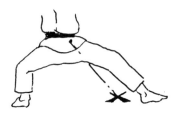

Kiba Dachi (straddled or horse stance)

Kiba dachi may be achieved by taking a step to the left and a step to the right from heiko dachi (parallel stance). Move feet from a.1 and b.1 to a.2 and b.2

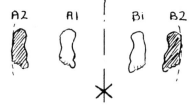

Bend the knees and push them sideways over the feet in position a.2 and b.2, keep the upper body straight and feel the hips pushing forwards and downwards to a point X on the floor. Kiba dachi is a very strong to the sides and can be used to execute techniques along this line. Yoko geri (side kick), gedan tsuki (low level strike), etc.

Notes to consider;

maintain upright position
force the knees outward, root yourself to the floor with the outside edges of your feet. flex the ankles to keep the knees in the correct position.
4) keep the hips low and pushed forward.

Stepping in Kiba dachi;
Form 1) To step with the back foot, in front of the leading foot, placing firmly onto the floor (do not obstruct the knee joint) as in a). Raise the left leg and step or raise the knee to chest to kick keage b).

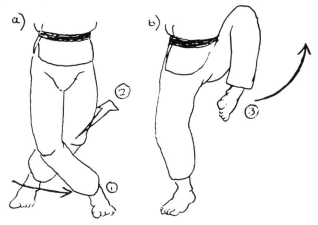

Form 2) For long range stepping, place the back foot behind the leading leg, pushing through with the hips for entrance. This is used in conjunction with yoko geri kekomi (side thrust kick), so as to use the full power of the hips and body weight.

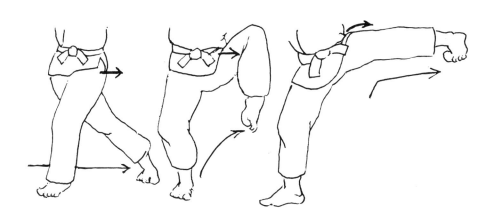

For strong stepping in kiba dachi draw the back leg upto, but not across, the front foot. Keep the hips low and the knees bent. Step with the front leg away from the back leg maintaining a constant hip height for maximum balance on entrance.

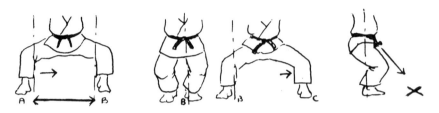

(Note; when moving to the left (the left is called the front), your right leg (is called the back).

Hangetsu Dachi (Half or crescent moon stance)

This is midway between front stance and a sanchin (hourglass) stance. The positions of the legs are similar to front stance, only shorter and the front foot is twisted in through forty-five degrees

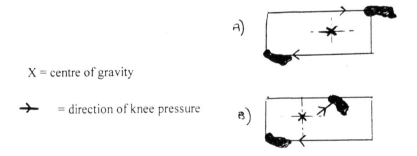

X = centre of gravity

➤ = direction of knee pressure

This stance is useful for both attack and defence. Because of the circular action of the front foot and knee it will avoid an oncoming attack with the first half of the circle and on completion would attack an opponents front leg joint, thus weakening their balance (diagram C). When stepping through, as in kata, one can feel a flowing rhythm in the step, which the blocks and punches can be related to, so that they finish at the same time as the step.

Bringing the rear leg up to the front leg, the weight is transferred to the front leg side, i.e. the whole body moves off the centre line of attack. The rear leg moves around the opponents attacking leg and circles inside the joint (knee). The opponents balance and on coming power is broken in the direction D.

It is good practice to perform all stances very slowly (as in tai chi), so that you can feel the transfer of body weight and centre of gravity. Thus studying when and where the legs can be lifted or the hips can move forward/ backward to the point of kime. From your early lessons you should be working on balance and stability for these are the foundation on which to build your techniques. Make the base area, produced by the feet as large as is practically possible. Keep the centre of gravity as near to the centre of the base. If your centre of gravity falls towards the outer limits of this base, balance will be broken.

This is the function of Hangetsu in this example. Destroy posture and the power of attack will also be destroyed.

Neko Ashi Dachi (Cat Foot Stance)

The centre of gravity is over the rear leg, so that either none or little weight is placed on the front foot. The latter foot placing Koshi (ball of the foot) on the floor. Although a stance in its own right, neko ashi can be found half way through many of the other stances. A mid point, shall we say, between stance A and stance B

ZENKUTSU ———> NEKO ASHI ———> HANGETSU

Neko ashi provides the opportunity to strike off the front leg e.g. mae geri. Or take short forward defensive steps keeping the same kicking leg forward for mae geri mae ashi. One could pull back from a long stance into neko ashi to create space, to avoid a strike or to pull an opponent off balance after a lunge or a grab at you. This posture may be incorporated in aiding a fast small turn to move around an attack without creating a large space between you and an assailant, allowing a quick counter attack at close range. Restricting any secondary attack from your opponent, as it would aid you to move inside the length of his arm. This posture would also help cover your groin area without a positive thought effort.

Tei no ji Dachi/ Cho ji Dachi (T-stance)

A ready posture similar to that of Aikido form. More upright and less committed to one side or the other, thus allowing you a wider range of counter positions. The centre of gravity is evenly placed, unlike cat stance where the weight is more over the rear leg.

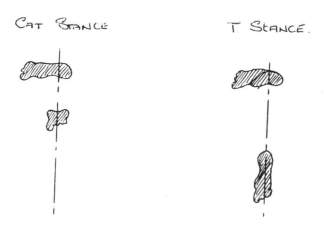

Fudo Dachi (Immovable Stance)

Similar to zenkutsu dachi except the rear is thrust forward and the hips are low at forty-five degrees. The body is leg is bent slightly, the stomach more comfortable for combat and therefore more relaxed. Remember I have said that stances are passed through, except at kime (sometimes), so if performed in kata this posture would allow a more flowing form.

Without posture and balance none of what follows can be delivered effectively, because as your techniques penetrate the opponent your body will give, sending a waste of energy backwards or away from the attack. A follow up, or secondary technique cannot be delivered either, until balance has been recovered.

Te Waza (Hand Techniques)

Seiken (Fore fist)

Is used to deliver a punch (tsuki), usually with the Knuckles of the index and middle fingers. At the moment of impact, tension should be concentrated in the little finger. This provides tension to the fist, but not to the whole forearm, allowing speed to be maintained to the point of impact. If the wrist is bent this will result in a loss of power and may lead to flexing of the joint and injury.

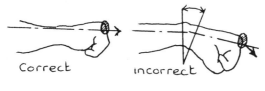

Correct   incorrect

Ippon Ken (Single Knuckle)

Provides a small penetrating striking surface, which is designed to go into the soft regions of the body. The eyes, neck, throat, and nerve points and the solar plexus being the classic targets. This technique can be delivered with tsuki (punch), or at the end of a uke (block) creating, or changing the technique to an uchi (strike). Ude uke would become ude uchi to disable the soft areas of the arm.

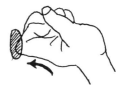

Nakadaka Ippon Ken (middle single knuckle)

Supported by fingers on both sides, it is a stronger knuckle, which can be used to provide a fast spinning or rotating strike deep under the skin layers, damaging nerve and muscle fibres.

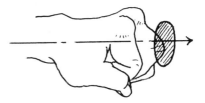

Uraken (Back Fist)

The fist is formed in the same manner as seiken, but the backs of the two knuckles are used instead of the front. Uraken is used to attack the opponents' face, side of head and neck, as well as the groin and inner thigh. Block with uraken inside the arm, or to the biceps to create a pause created by discomfort and pain.

Tetsui (Bottom of Fist)

Here the bottom of the fist is used to strike the target. With a snap and twist of the forearm. Used to attack the bridge of the nose or top of the head. Down and back into the groin and round into the kidneys. Double Tetsui to the floating ribs, as in the middle of Bassai Dai kata.

Shuto (Knife Hand)

When using the Shuto hand a feeling of energy
must flow into the fingers, so that they are tense
and strong. Keep the fingers close together, each
acting as a support or splint for the others. Lead
with the thumb and twist through impact. Use the
outer edge of the hand to block/ strike the opponents
arm, neck etc. When using as a strike, snap the
forearm outwards from the elbow or drop the body
weight to break balance, if leading into a throw.
Do not over straighten, move the body forwards
to make up distance.

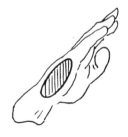

Haito (Ridge Hand)

This technique employs the area slightly below
the base of the index finger to the first joint of
the thumb, and is delivered with a roundhouse
action, or an ude uke action with an inverted palm.
Used to the ear, temple, neck, floating ribs,
groin and inside of the thigh.

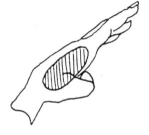

Haishu (Back Hand)

Uses the area of the hand from the knuckles
to the point where the hand and wrist connects.
Used to strike the face, side of neck, arm,
groin or ear. As a block, as in Heine Yodan
to jodan or as a sweeping action under a punch

Koken (Bent Wrist)

The hand is bent down to its maximum,
fingers and thumb tips brought together.
The top surface of the wrist is used to strike
and block. Used to strike under the jaw,
strike triceps, elbow (when extended), groin, inner thigh, inner calf or ankle.

Nuki te (Spear hand)

The points of the fingers form a reasonable
level surface. Keeping them close together
the fingers may be used to attack the solar plexus,
the eyes, the armpit, nerve areas and soft tissue.

Empi (Elbow)

May be executed as a straight thrust
with the body weight **A)**,
or circular, similar to the European
fore arm smash **B)**,
except the elbow and the
forearm combine for maximum
penetration

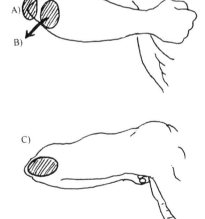

One can also use the back of the
upper arm from the elbow to the bottom
of the triceps **C).**
Delivered in reverse roundhouse form

Taisho (Palm Heel)

Block or strike with the fleshy
palm of the hand. Pushing or
parrying action or thrusting as in,
up under the nose or striking the chin.
Invert fingers downward for low level
strike to the groin as in Heine godan.

Leg Strike (areas)

Koshi (Ball of the Foot)

Is used by many Karateka, because
it is a powerful and a small area provides
penetration with the front kick and
roundhouse kick. It also provides
extension beyond the shin If someone
should block you there (Fig 1).

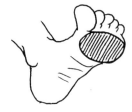

(Fig1)

Sokuto (Ridge of the foot)

Used as the striking area for a side kick
(Yoko Geri). The edge is narrow and provides
good penetration into the stomach or ribs.
It can also rise to chop up under the armpit.
Also used with reversed crescent kick
(Gyaku Mikazuki) to strike the inside of
the bicep or the shoulder joint.

Haisoku (Instep)

Is very common in contest karate because it can be used with the popular roundhouse kick. It is easily controlled and the fact that it does not penetrate makes it safer than Koshi. This area of the foot is used with kin geri and forms of ashi barai etc. Remember you are striking with the small bones in the top of the foot and caution should be taken during practice.

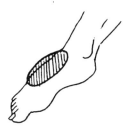

Hizagashira/ Hiza Geri (Knee Kick)

Used at close quarters, as with Empi. A short powerful technique, delivering the point of the patella (kneecap), to the groin, stomach, face, and elbow or inside of thigh. There is also mawashi hiza geri, a roundhouse form of delivery, usually to the floating ribs.

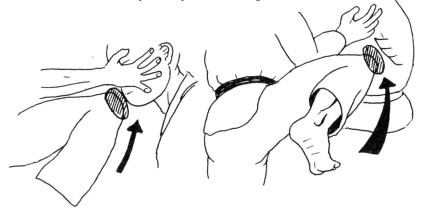

Kakato (The Heel)

Used in Kakato geri (fig 1), a form of mae geri kekomi, a thrust or horizontal drive where the knee is raised high, and allowed to drop, thus pushing the leg our straight. This can be likened to lifting the leg up and then along the top of a table, or kicking someone standing behind a chair. The strike is usually to the stomach or groin. This part of the foot may also be used in the axe type kick, usually only seen in the movies.

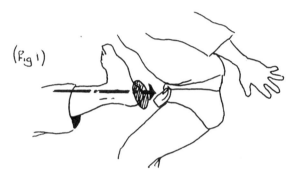

(Fig 1)

When executing the back-spinning roundhouse (Ushiro Mawashi Geri), the kime point is focused through the heel, Kakato (fig 2)

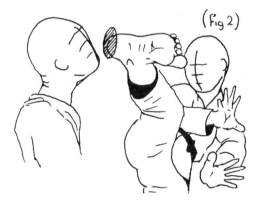

(Fig 2)

Also used when stamping to the side of the knee, onto the opponents' foot and even striking to the shin if held from the rear. Or the calf muscle when executing an Osotogari (a sweeping or reaping throw).

Blocking

This is the art of deflection, posture breaking and creating pain as a means to alter the opponent's line of thought and offence i.e. momentum.

Gedan Barai (Low level block/ sweep)

Because students are taught to execute this technique "as a block" from the shoulder, they believe that it must always be delivered from this point. It should be explained that the block follows a line running from the shoulder and the forearm cuts a diagonal downwards, across the body to finish in a striking punch-like action over the knee, knuckles facing the opponent. This will achieve a cutting punch like action through the opponent's arm at forty-five degrees and not ninety as is often practiced. Training in the latter encourages use of the arm only. Whereas the whole body and hara should be applied.

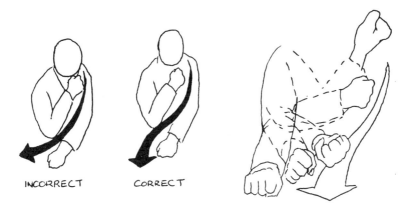

INCORRECT   CORRECT

The most important point, is that by practising this technique continuously from the basic position, the student is only learning the line of attack. So that when understood and your brain has absorbed the memory and feeling of the line, your defensive attack should be able to fall onto that line at any point. One should also be able to maintain its feeling and effectiveness.

This basic idea follows into every one of the techniques and should be remembered. Power is provided by the combination of the twist and the body movement forwards and down, which should come to the kime (focus point) at the same time.

When blocking a low or middle level punch note that because the force of the bodyweight and feeling from the hips is down and forward and incorporates the twist of the arm towards the opponents hip. The result should be a breaking of his posture, in the lower spinal region of his back.

Maximum pressure, posture broken, and his secondary technique is In effective

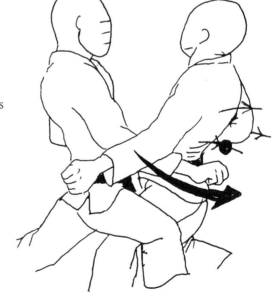

This feeling must also apply whether moving forwards or backwards to defend. In other words, although moving backwards, at the point of kime, your hips, knee and weight should be of a forward motion. This is achieved by briefly moving back into a Kokutsu, or Fudo dachi and flowing forwards into your opponent with your knee and hip. Where possible always move off the line of attack.

1) Ready
2) Drop back into Kokutsu dachi
3) Spiral down + forward.

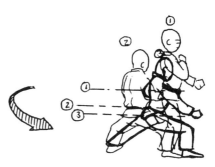

In effect a U-turn is achieved at the hip level A back and forward flow, created by the knees and focused at Hara (and the wrist & hand)

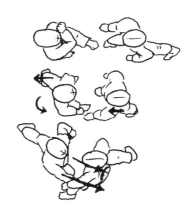

Ude Uke (Middle outer block)

From basic form, the defending hand moves from the hip and takes the shortest route to protect the body. This is a diagonal line e.g. from the right hip forwards and upwards until the elbow passes across the solar plexus (giving it forearm protection). Keeping the hand above and more importantly forward of the elbow, to maintain a strong forward action capable of resisting strength purely by the defenders body weight.
If the hand is square or behind the elbow the attacking part of the block will become weak and dependent on the strength in the shoulders. (This use of upper body strength could result in a breaking of your posture).
Once the elbow has covered the centre of the body and the hand has passed beyond the centre line the elbow snaps back to its own right side. The hand follows, travelling slightly forwards to penetrate or jab through the opponent's arm on a forward diagonal and the wrist twists into an inverted punch-like action.

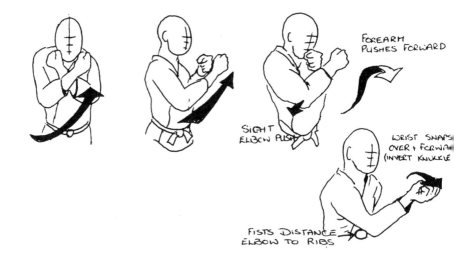

FOREARM PUSHES FORWARD

SIGHT ELBOW PUSH

WRIST SNAPS OVER + FORWARD (INVERT KNUCKLE)

FISTS DISTANCE ELBOW TO RIBS

The striking action of the knuckles, whilst twisting, are forwards and slightly downwards. Striking the edge of the attacking wrist and following through towards the upper arm (base of bicep). It can also be delivered as a direct strike (note when striking do not over straighten the arm or you become weak at the elbow. It would be easy to apply a lock or break e.g. wan kan setsu (straight arm lock). The floating ribs would also be open to attack.

Age Uke (Rising or Upper Level Block)

Again, taking the technique from its basic form it should be thrust, fist first, from the hip diagonally upwards towards the opponents' face. (a relaxed clenched fist with palm uppermost). The punch approaches the attacking arm and the wrist rotates to deliver a slicing punch. The fist glances past the arm, so that the wrist provides a glancing blow that continues through. The result is a wedge like action taking the oncoming attack off at an angle. At this point the technique is complete, or you may strike the side of his jaw if you a) you continue through, or b) he has come through with some force.
During all blocking techniques the body weight and centre of gravity should move forward and down. The strength and power of the technique comes from the body and its directional weight, and not from the strength of the arms.
Because low and upper level blocks have more arm extension in basic form, the feeling of tsuki should be very strong with the elbow driving through behind the fist. Always aim through the target; in fact concentrate your focus several inches beyond. Make sure the shoulders are relaxed, the back is straight
and the stomach is pushing forward to maintain balance and posture.

It is important to note that when in negative direction and broken posture, none of your techniques can be powerful (at this stage), the negative force counter acts them.

Always think forty five degrees with age uki

Pushing from the hip for entrance breaks posture and attack. Turning his force into negative direction.

Shuto Uke (Knife hand)

Believed to be one of the most devastating techniques, yet the most difficult to develop. We shall begin with the arm across the body ready to block (fig a). again the elbow is in front of the solar plexus. The hand is situated vertically above the elbow, the thumb/ ridge is twisted to the front and the palm is facing the head. The fingers are straight, tense and pushed together. The other arm is situated under the elbow of the first, palm open to cover the ribs or extended to parry a first strike.

(fig a)

(fig a)

Shuto commences to travel forwards
Diagonally across the body (leading
With the thumb). The hand and elbow
travel forward and across. The elbow
slides over the back of the second arm and hand.

At this point the hand will be ready to make contact with the offensive wrist. Here your wrist twists violently bringing the rest of the hand past the thumb. The hand and elbow travel slightly downwards, the knife-edge slicing into its target. (Note: it is a slice like a knife, not a chop like an axe). Now the wrist snaps forward to penetrate into the nerve or muscle of the arm (forearm or bicep usually).

During this process the stomach and hips are rotating and pushing downwards and forwards, the knees bending as in Kokutsu.

This technique is used to the inside, or the outside of the arm, the bicep, triceps or forearm, shoulder joint, neck, head, wrist, inside thigh, knee joint, foot ankle and inverted to the groin.

Shuto can be used in an arc like covering action, when incorporated with a spinning body movement like tae-sabaki for avoidance. One can also move outside an arm, whilst moving in to apply an arm lock (gyaku wan kan setsu) or a pressure point to the vagus nerve or cartoid mastoid in the neck.

ROTATION AT KIMÉ

This technique can be used in either acceptance (Tenkan), the enveloping circular form, or the rejective (Irimi) entering form, which are adapted from the Aikido aspects of movement and energy, to be covered later.

SHUTO PERFORMED IN TENKAN.

Uchi Komi (Inner winding)

A technique, which at basic level, begins with the blocking arm being driven upwards (like a punch). Vertically past the side of the head, with the thumb twisted to the front. The second hand positioning at forty-five degrees forwards of chudan (resembling a short diagonal jab). Providing temporary cover for the solar plexus. The blocking hand begins to spiral down from above the head, keeping the elbow directly below it, until it reaches the centre line of the chest. Once at the centre or the line of the attack, the direction and feeling alters to become a snapping, rotating inverted forward punch. (The feeling of movement should be of holding a staff, and swinging it down and around with both hands. The hand holding the top of the pole being the block (or strike) and the hand holding the lower part of the pole returning to the hip.

The hand twists and with a short snapping action rotates. The knuckles can strike, or a single knuckle strike like ippon ken or nakadaka ken can be used into the shoulder or between the bicep and triceps to deaden the softer regions of the arm. These moves are combined with rotation of the hips, which will add power, without the necessity for over tension in the forearms.

Taisho (Palm Heel)

In basic form taisho follows the straight attack or block with the arm, usually bent through the elbow at ninety or forty five degrees from the body. This then acts as a flat palming off or parrying movement.

But taisho is best effective as a flat striking action when it has the force of the hip behind it. When stepping into, or passing through kiba dachi (horse stance), the flow produced from the rotating hip that so increases the force of the hand technique from that hip that penetration into chudan (middle) level can be achieved with very little power or arm movement. (refer to Jion Kata). Taisho can be used to all levels and vital areas. Upper levels are struck with the fingers uppermost (A1), whilst lower level techniques are done with the fingers inverted (A2).

Osai Uke (Pressing Block)

Using the taisho palm heel, this block presses down (either forwards or back) against a punch, normally a secondary or counter attack.
In basics, if you have blocked with shuto, the opponent may throw a gyaku tsuki. Your shuto (leading hand) may then press the punch down (Heine or Pinan nidan as a classic example of this).
If the knees and hips lower together, the attackers balance will be driven forwards into the ground. We can now see why in Kata it is followed by a nukite (spear hand), not to the chest, but to his face or throat because he has been taken down to his knees.

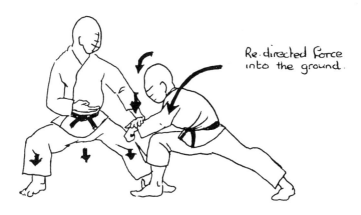

Re-directed force into the ground.

When the whole body drops to block the effect is dramatic.

Juji Uke (Cross Block)

Used at various levels this technique takes on several variations of open or clenched fist, but many students remain on the line of attack, believing it to be strong. The technique is used against a snap kick or a downward strike (perhaps with a weapon), so it is a good practice to move off line and attack from the hips.

In order to develop imagery use gedan barai and gedan seiken punch combination to feel kime. A feeling of blocking the leg with gedan barai, whilst striking the shin simultaneously. Use gedan as previously described and seiken from the shoulder with the elbow directly behind. At low level grade move off the striking line, (never be at the end of a technique). Do not lean forwards, but rather push from the hips and allow a gap from the hands to the groin, in order to avoid the kyoshi foot position (remember this foot covers more area than heisoku).

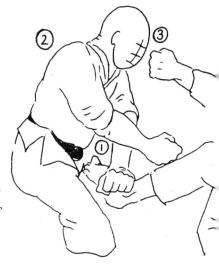

Good block but?

1) Still on attack line and struck in groin
2) Leaning forwards creates bad posture, Restricts movement and
3) Throwing head forward will result in you blocking with your nose or your eye (Ouch!!!)

Haito (Ridge Hand)

Can be used in a similar way as ude uke, and from the same basic start
positions. It can be seen in this form in Jutte (Jitte). As a strike, say to
jodan, it could be delivered with a mawashi action (palm down on
impact). As an option it can also be used with a tae-sabaki movement.
This technique is used Repeatedly in Unsu kata in a repeated wave of
attacks both forward (mae) and to the rear (ushiro).

Haishu (Back of Hand)

As in Heine Yodan it can be used to block an attack to the head. It is still
important however to remember the twist at the striking point, so that the
technique may travel out from the hip with the palm facing down.
Because the hand is behind the elbow with this method the second hand
defends the face and the attack may appear like a scissor action of the
arms. This of course is just one variation of many often covered whilst in
Kokutsu dachi covering the side. As in shuto, the thumb may lead out to
provide the twist at kime. In Heine Yodan one feels the hands are grabbed
at the wrists. Here if one projects through the fingers and turns the whole
body to the side, the opponents attack is over balanced. You can swing
the arms up

to jodan and breaks his grip with the rotating and opening of the arms. With practice this version provides a feeling of Ki projection or force, which can relate to the other more direct hand techniques.

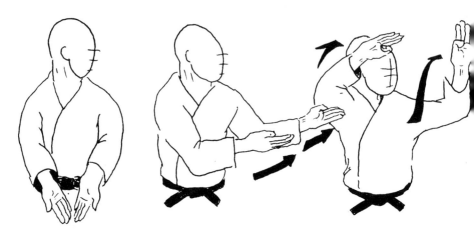

Body movement and hand movement in synchronisation for maximum kime to ensure defence against a powerful roundhouse (either hand or foot). Here we see an example of two directional blocking, i.e. the side and front. Although different levels can be covered only jodan is seen here.

There are of course other blocks and techniques to be covered, although at this stage it would create to many facts, feelings and exercises to be deemed practical. Cover everything to date both in terms of Irimi and tenkan, stepping forwards and backwards and feeling from Hara (the point just below the naval), and your technique and kata practice has just doubled or trebled. Practice as slow as possible to feel the posture and develop the balance through the stances and co-ordinate mind and body and bring your breathing in time. Breathe out through several techniques and use open extended hands to perform "liquid" movement.

In basics bring the hips, steps, blocks and strikes into a single motion. At this stage forget completely about speed of the body. Only speed in the twisting of the wrist is important to develop the snap of the block or strike, it is this that makes them the same. "A punch is a block, a block is a punch". This feeling is all-important. Once understood speed can be added as a bonus.

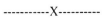

-----------X----------

Striking

Many students in many styles practice striking after the step. From the previous chapters you will know my feelings for the strike to finish with the body movement. This feeling of kime combined with entrance enables penetration to the internal organs. Attacking the surface of the body is a futile exercise, and a tiring one. Physics tells us that for every action, there is and equal and opposite reaction, and this cannot be seen in any better arena than the Martial way. The force of the tsuki punch as it comes from the rotation of the hips produces an opposite reaction, which is expelled in the same instant through the empi. We have produced a piston like action of the arms when striking and blocking whilst rigid. When the hips rotate with all of the body this can still apply. Try stepping in kiba dachi with taisho to the front and empi to the rear.

We can now consider a circular movement with all the energy transferred through the opponent. This requires the circle to finish with a forward body movement.

LINE OF ATTACK

50% ENERGY IN

50° ENERGY "OUT" (WASTAGE)

Side step and move forward, in stance, but in the manner of a kendoka. Front leg to the side and forward, as the back leg manoeuvres offline the hip centre rotates and moves forward through the Hara centre.

Don't allow the non-attacking side of the hips to rotate away from your opponent.

You should have closed the gap between you and your attacker. On the rotation and the locking of the arm, it should drive through to the back of the opponent. Passing through the front, as the hips locks down and forwards.

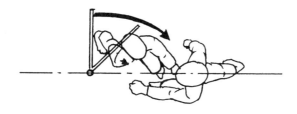

ENERGY AND MOTION SHOULD TRAVEL
FORWARD 100% FROM ANY GIVEN SIDE.
THIS PRODUCES A 'SLAMMIN DOOR' EFFECT.
WITH POSITIVE ENERGY (NO NEGATIVE)

Your opponent should be knocked back on impact or re-directed. You should not jump or be bounced away from him (this is negative energy). This feeling should apply to oi tsuki. gyaku tsuki, nukite, taisho, empi, mawashi tsuki, shuto uchi etc, and allow us to move into throws, wrist and arm locks or any technique or movement where body contact is required at, or after the kime point.

Geri Waza (Kicking Techniques)

Karate excels itself beyond western forms of fighting because it incorporates the extra length and power of the legs to their fullest potential. One sensei described karate to me, as the art of dirty fighting, because of the unexpected and well-developed use of the legs. If we consider ourselves to be fighters then I have to agree. To be a fighter of the highest level one should use every weapon at his disposal to defend himself. The legs are one of the most obvious and best weapons not only for long range but multi directional attacks. A disadvantage however, is that to an un-skilled karateka, using his legs may risk him loosing balance, or being swept or thrown, or being pushed, simply because he is left supported only by a single limb.

Hiza geri (Knee Kick)

Although a strike in its own right, this is also the first basic part of a front kick. It involves raising the knee to chest level, whilst lowering posture by slightly bending the supporting leg. The foot is pointed downwards, but the toes are drawn back. From this position a front snap kick (keage) could be delivered easily.

This part of the movement, the raisin and lowering must be practiced, in order that the speed can be built up without injury. Suppleness must be developed in the hip joint and the thigh muscles must be trained and conditioned. Without speed from the floor to the chest, no kick would be effective.

It would only be a weak swing of the leg. Strength and balance are obtained with slow motion practice. From front stance pull with the front knee, so that the body weight is brought over the front leg. Keeping the back straight and pushing from hara raise the back leg into a thrusting knee position.

Bend the supporting leg for balance and to take the pressure on the muscles and not the joint. Now thrust the hip and knee into the target. Feeling can be increased by extending the hands, as if grabbing an opponent

head. Synchronise the thrust of the hips forwards with the pulling of the hands back to produce an equal/ opposite action

Mawashi Hiza Geri (Roundhouse Knee Kick)

From a front stance bring the knee up to the side, raising the striking hip and thrusting it forward to drive the knee into the target. During the thrust turn the supporting knee and foot outward to aid with rotation and balance.

Should you extend your hands for feeling during this technique both hands will be pulled back to either

A) The thrusting hip and the body should be in "Hanmi" half facing at forty five degrees to the attack.

B) Past both sides of the knee

(Fig A)   (Fig B)   Rear view

Mae Geri, Kekomi (Front Kick, Thrusting)

Here is a most powerful and penetrating technique, which all too often puts the kicker at risk. Simply because he lacks the balance and control in the supporting leg to recover posture after the kime point, and may be caught falling forward to put the kicking leg on the floor. The result being, that the leg may be taken away by a sweeping action of the opponents foot (Ashi Barai).

When kicking one should keep the supporting leg slightly bent (using the universal flex of the knee for balance and stability). The weight of the hips and lower abdomen correctly balanced over this. On extending the leg, if it were pushed to far, it would result in a loss of balance and no secondary technique could follow, should it be required. This "over thrust" extends through the groin and the kicker ends up with only the ball of the foot as a means of support (Fig 1).

Poor technique with full commitment,

Allowing no balance for secondary technique.

One should keep the supporting foot firmly on the floor and again keep the centre of gravity low for stability. The knee of the kicking leg should be brought high, so that the chest is covered, but more importantly so that the thrusting foot can travel out horizontally to the opponents mid section, aiming for the spine through the stomach wall. The kicker should lower the hips and push forward (fractionally) before contact to increase the momentum of the thrust through the small striking area of Koshi (ball of the foot).

One should practice kicking over a chair or table and pulling back as an aid to developing strength of thigh, balance and control (Fig 2)

Good posture with bent support knee,
Hip entrance, but knee can push or pull
Back for secondary kick or trap.

GOOD POSTURE

Front Kick, Snapping (Mae Geri, Keage)

This kick is used at close quarters and works with a hinging action of the knee to snap the foot
upwards, whilst the thrust of the hips drives the foot forwards. It may be used to strike the groin, inner
thigh, even an elbow joint after it has been trapped or locked, although the latter is not a common
option. When done at speed it can break or dislocate the knee or rupture the groin or stomach wall.
Normally today however it is more likely to be as a flick, which will stun the opponent ready for a secondary attack (Fig s1).

Fig s1

Fig s2

The kick (as all kicks) can be delivered with the back leg, or from the front leg, when half a step is used Mae Geri Mae Ashi (front kick front foot), as in Fig s2. The kick is fast and powerful and uses the weight of the whole body moving forwards.

Recoil the leg immediately after impact o the position prior to the snap i.e. the knee remains constant from the start of the snap to the recoil. Keeping the knee at this height allows greater variety in your next move e.g. kick mawashi geri, step forwards or backwards, lunge and punch, grab and rotate into Tae Otoshi throw.

After all kicks, the knee should be treated in this manner. Never fall forwards, but place the foot down and pass through neko ashi or cho ji dachi, sliding forwards to maximise posture, stability and fluidity on a horizontal line.

The centre of the hips should never undulate. This rise and fall of the hips would be used, perhaps by a judoka or aikidoka to aid in throwing and countering and it is also a waste of energy thus tiring the legs.

Side Kick, Thrusting (Yoko Geri, Keage)

From basic front stance the sidekick can be delivered in several ways. The feeling being different according to the delivery and direction required. The following descriptions are based on kicking with the back leg, bur as with mae geri, the front leg could be used with the stepping up of the rear leg.

Kicking with the back leg will incorporate the principals of hip entrance and rotation, pulling with the front knee and keeping hara on a horizontal line. Having brought the knee up to the chest or chudan level the forms begin to differ

1) Facing your opponent raise the foot to the height of the knee and perform mae geri kekomi until the thrust is almost delivered. At this point the supporting foot and leg twists to the side and the hips rotate (the hip of the kicking leg now being over the hip of the supporting leg). At this same time the

foot of the thrusting leg rotates, the big toe is pulled back and the edge of
the foot is driven through with the heel first.

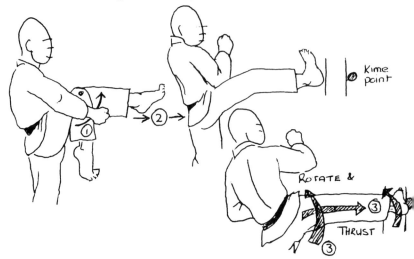

11) On raising the knee to the chest, attempt to keep the foot directly
underneath it. Rotate the body through ninety degrees, so that this
combined action is visualised as a deflecting block with the shin,
taking the offensive limb past the side of ones body. Raise the foot to
knee height and thrust out sideways and slightly backwards until the heel
of the foot strikes its target.

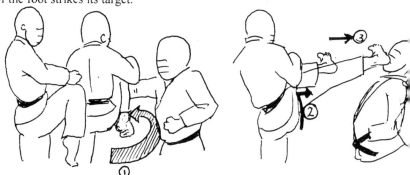

Rotate and pivot hips. Knee high to block   **raise foot to knee height and thrust**

Due to the rotation the thrust must travel slightly to the rear to produce kime in line with the buttocks, thus producing a triangular configuration of movement to the face, chest or down to the abdomen or hip joint.

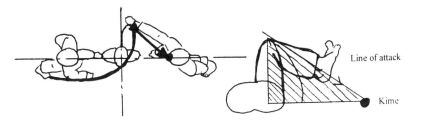

Line of attack

Kime

111) The third build-up to yoko geri is based on the circumstance of your opponent attacking from the side e.g. like heine/ pinan nidan, or yodan, although in these kata keage is used. The option is to raise the back leg and kick or half step with this leg to bring it under the centre of gravity (for balance), and so allow the front leg to be lifted to hiza geri position to the front. Raise the foot and hip sideways and deliver the thrust back onto the line of the buttocks (as in (11)). The knee is drawn back to the chest ready to step down or perform a secondary kick Fumikomi (stamping) for example.

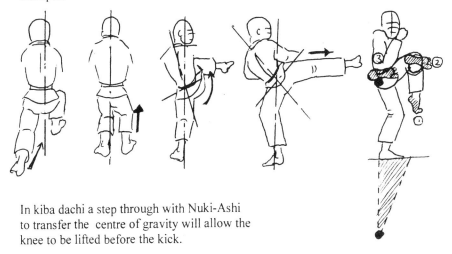

In kiba dachi a step through with Nuki-Ashi to transfer the centre of gravity will allow the knee to be lifted before the kick.

Side kick snapping (Yoko Geri Keage)

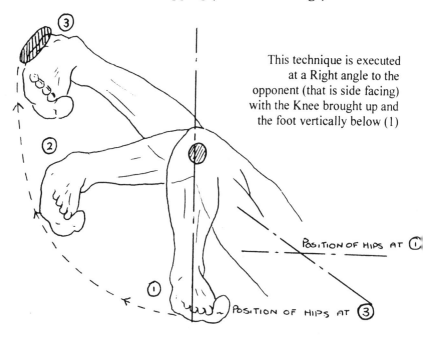

This technique is executed at a Right angle to the opponent (that is side facing) with the Knee brought up and the foot vertically below (1)

POSITION OF HIPS AT ①

POSITION OF HIPS AT ③

The front hip is raised or tilted through the kick, to bring the centre of gravity over the supporting leg. The knee remains high and acts as a hinge as the foot sweeps upward to defend or attack. Keep the edge of the foot uppermost and use the heel as the focus point. Attacks are usually delivered to the underside of the chin, arm, and elbow or into the armpit. The leg does NOT have to lock straight, as penetration at the kime point results from the speed and thrust in the swing and lock of the hips. This move is performed in tekki kata and heine nidan and yodan. Here there is a simultaneous uraken strike to jodan. Our teaching and training involves a mental image of striking an area the size of a tennis ball (at Jodan). This then focuses the hand and foot on a single striking point e.g. like hitting the side and bottom of the mandible at the same time. This practice will stop the uraken sweeping upwards and will develop a forward drive, not negative (backwards), in the upper body.

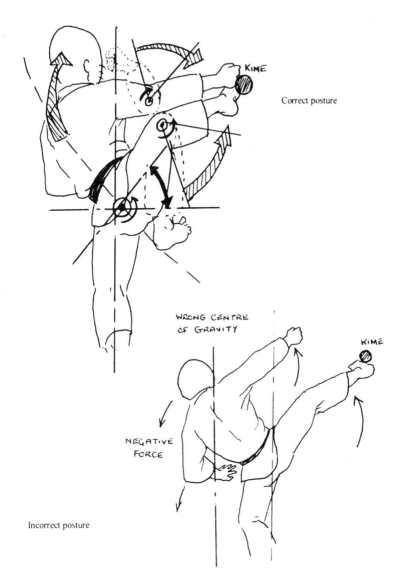

KIME

Correct posture

WRONG CENTRE
OF GRAVITY

KIME

NEGATIVE
FORCE

Incorrect posture

Wrong mental and visual feeling results in a loss of posture and balance, when practising without a

physical target.

Crescent Kick (Mikazuki Geri)

Is said to be an application of the roundhouse kick. "Mikazuki" means crescent moon, but also translates as "new", the new kick would suggest it was added sometime later than the traditional kicks.
Mikazuki takes on several forms too, and is delivered from a variety of postures e.g. ready stance, front stance, cat stance and horse stance.

Form 1. The defending leg swings upwards in an arc across the body. The toes are turned upward and the block is made with the sole of the foot (straight or bent knee can be used at kime). Distance and height of the oncoming attack will determine the leg, knee and foot positions. After the block, which can hit the attack at ninety degrees, or hook to bring the opponent into you, the knee is kept high, so that you are ready to stamp down or kick (or slide out into stance).

Form 2. If the foot is raised higher than the attack it can be brought down on top of it, re directing it's
 force toward the ground. Here the hips are more turned and the knee more through, and over the top of
the attackers arm or leg.

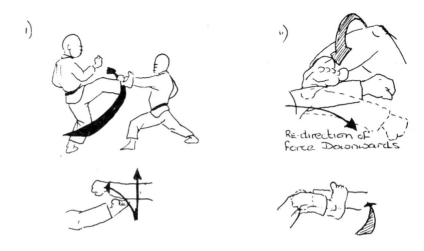

Form 3. Mikazuki can be used as a strike. with a locking action and forty five-degree drive into the shoulder joint for example. This is an advanced form, which requires practice for balance and accurate timing to destroy the opponents' momentum and posture.

In 3b it should be noted that the defender has moved off the line of attack. Never stop on your opponents' pre arranged kime point, because if your defence fails your body movement will prevent damage. It also provides weight and directional force to attack or rotate. One then has the option of using tenkan or irimi as a by-product. (We shall look at this principal in another chapter).

Roundhouse Kick (Mawashi Geri)

In this form of kicking speed and power are evident. This is wasted in many competitions however, because it is nearly always delivered to jodan with the foot travelling upwards, with the bodyweight rising. Concentration in this chapter will be given to the kick being delivered from the front stance, although, as with other kicks it can be delivered from others (kiba dachi, neko ashi dachi etc).

Bring up the back leg to the side, with the knee driving through in the bent, locked position and the foot tucked up behind the buttock (fig 1). When kicking with Migi (right), the body should rotate ninety degrees to the left and the knee is driven forwards using the force from this twist. Keep the knee higher than the foot initially, as dropping the knee to early restricts the height and the power of the kick. It may also result with the back being exposed (fig 2).

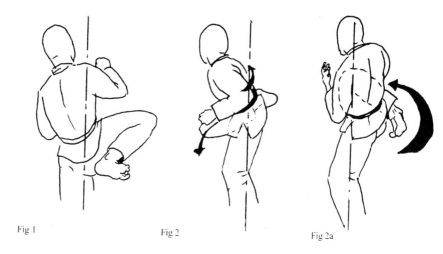

Fig 1   Fig 2   Fig 2a

From the correct position Fig2a, the foot should travel up to the required height, arcing away from the buttocks. Before contact the body s rotating to the left and the knee circles, the foot locking into position (either horizontal or the toes slightly below the heel). On contact the foot should be travelling slightly downwards, thus allowing the weight of the leg to be used to the maximum, but be sure the knee has not dropped. Open the legs as wide as possible and strike the target at a right angle. Many students and yudansha bring the knee of the striking leg level with the hip and then snap out the foot. This serves to flick or slap the target (Fig 3).

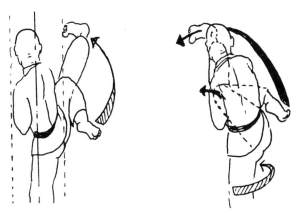

Fig 3   Fig 4

Take the front knee through the centre line, so that the Koshi strike penetrates. Taking the knee beyond the centre line also serves as an obstacle between the opponent and your stomach and solar plexus, floating ribs and groin.

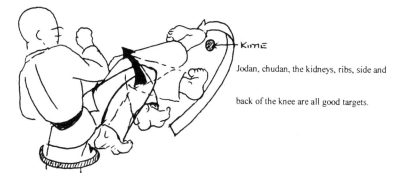

Kime

Jodan, chudan, the kidneys, ribs, side and

back of the knee are all good targets.

Back Kick (Ushiro Geri)

When breaking down the series of movements in this technique it may seem complicated, however that is compensated by the total defensive posture achieved throughout. At the beginning it is essential to explain ashi barai (foot sweep), as it is used at the outset of ushiro geri (Ushiro mawashi geri also).

From front stance the body weight is transferred to the back leg, either by taking a half step forward with the rear leg, or moving back, so that the weight is transferred. In either case or depending on the scenario the hips rotate forwards, so that the front leg turns across the body and the foot finishes at forty five to sixty degrees to the rear. The foot is effectively hooking around the attackers front leg. This sweep takes the opponent's foot in the direction it is already travelling i.e. forwards. Because it's grip and resistance is least effective. The results can vary, from a broken posture and a loss of balance to full splits.

Break posture with ashi barai.

The foot turn, helped with the rotation of the hip and tenkan of ones arm brings the weight back through the front leg at the mid-point. Continue to circle or rotate and raise the back leg. As the pivot continues lower the ones torso and head and thrust back with the leg, locking it and keeping the foot as vertical as possible, thus striking with the heel.

By pulling back with the hip and the upper body, one could keep distance or move away from an attack as the front foot is turned at forty-five degrees. Rotation remains as before, so the hips now change to a forward direction to drive into the oncoming attacker.

Rotation allows acceptance through one side
and rejects through the other like a revolving door

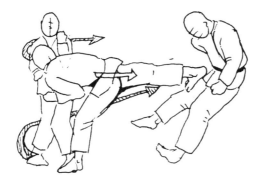

Pull back and rotate left hip away from the opponent, changing body weight through the right hip putting force back towards the opponent.

Jumping/ Flying Front Kick (Tobi Mae Geri)

From front or natural stance (Fudo dachi) the rear leg is thrown forwards and upwards, with a feeling of stepping onto a high stool. Hips and body continue the drive, so that the supporting leg is lifted from the ground. This second knee is driven up past the first and the foot is snapped out (keage), or thrust out after much practice (kekomi). After the kime point, the first leg will have started returning to the floor, regaining balance through the flex of the knee. The kicking leg should be pulled back to the chest position (prior to it striking) as we should assume we need to hold balance and kick out a second time with the same leg as a stamping, side or roundhouse.

Posture   control   and balance

You should land like a cat, soft and light and remaining balanced on one leg as an exercise.

Reverse Roundhouse Kick (ushiro Mawashi Geri)

As with ushiro geri the rotation is started in the same manner. The use of
the uchi komi, ashi barai combination throws the leading hip into its spin.
Here though, the body stays as upright as possible, and the head and upper
torso twists a) to see the opponent and b) to protect the opposite side of the
body as it takes over the rotation leading into the kick. The leg raises heel
first and at the chosen height, either hooks across the opponent with Kakato
(heel), or arcs horizontally locking and focusing through the centre point of
impact.

Try to ensure all momentum is towards the opponent by drawing the hips,
head and shoulders forward. Control is demonstrated by pulling the
kicking foot back, so that it comes to rest under the knee. The hips are
low and the muscles take the pressure off the supporting knee joint by
keeping it bent. This must be truly understood before the next technique
is practiced.

Jumping Back Roundhouse Kick
(Tobi Ushiro mawashi Geri)

"Kime as the leg locks",
at the apex of the jump

Springing from a Hachi dachi (natural stance),
side facing, the body rotates and the knees are brought up,
as if to jump over a low sweeping staff. The head, body and hips rotating
to perform a one hundred and eighty-degree turn.
But the leg snaps out to connect the heel with the opponent's jaw.
Momentum of the foot striking horizontally at ninety degrees to the target
and the body rotation provides the force. Centrifugal force will normally
carry the leg all the way back to the rear, but if contact is made, then it is
unlikely that this would occur. Practice until a soft landing can be
performed. A single error will send you sprawling to the floor. Throughout
remain fully relaxed to maximise height, speed and consequently balance.

Every technique to this point should now be combined, in a flowing motion from one to another, breathing slowly, in order that several moves can be performed to one slow exhalation. This is called Kihon and is practiced in a straight line, so that you only have to focus on the techniques.
Develop patterns of block, punch and kick to determine the correctness of posture and movement through the hips and eventually move from straight to rotating forms. Be slow where possible to feel the shifting centre of gravity. If one adopts this mental attitude to kihon and progresses onto kata, the spiritual aspects of "Ki" will manifest themselves. In today's arena speed is emphasised in kata, but one should perform at a speed where kata take several minutes or more, similar to Tai Chi, and it is far more beneficial onto the brains circuits. Only then should speed be increased.

---------X--------

Kata

A kata may be regarded as a combination of defensive and offensive techniques, but it is more than just that. One should try to develop the feelings and understanding, indeed the very spirit of the time, when Masters sat down to create the kata.

One should develop mental imagery, fluidity, balance, power and an understanding of acceptance as well as the common rejection to produce a realistic form. Without these elements the kata is purely a dance, a superficial act to impress the spectator and satisfy the ego.

The aim of the kata is to bring the body and the spirit into one entity. With understanding comes the concentrated power, the continuity of breathing, so there is no interruption of movement.

It is important to remember that appearances can be deceptive. Where the student is taught the purely physical, external power and tension, then it will be difficult to comprehend that a weak-looking, soft and relaxed technique, where the power is focused, is capable of penetrating almost anything.

Practising slowly develops the understanding of energy flow e.g. from rear posture into front posture, where the centre of gravity travels forwards through "hara", to be pushed out from the knee, hip and rotation of the punch or block. This overall flow of the total body mass cannot be compared with the force from an arm or a leg only (even where hip twist applies). Many masters teach that a tired student will perform kata, and technique generally, better than one who will is fresh. Indeed these masters would make their students perform a single kata ten, twenty or even fifty times without stopping. Eventually tension and stiffness will cease and pure flowing technique will remain. Technique controlled by fluidity and force, not from physical strength and stiffness.

Aikido teaches us much about flowing body movement and stepping, and introduced me to the principals of circular technique to my overall knowledge. This feeling, when added to kata, opened up a whole new image of defensive form and posture to the routines. The movement of the hips in aiding escape movements and applying wrist locks e.g. Tekki kata, Heine nidan. Rotating body movements as in Kanku dai and Jutte. Breaking the posture of ones opponent as in the very first move of Heine nidan and kanku dai (from a grab), or with the hand sweeping away a kick demonstrated in Bassai dai.

For years kata have been faithfully practiced by students and teachers alike. But today teachers are dropping off the routines because they fail to understand the movements, and so assume they have no function. Surely every twist of a wrist, every turn and rotation has a purpose. One should perform the kata thinking about the meaning and the function, even interpreting them in your own way. Use this as an excersise to broaden the mind and focus conscious motion to defend against all possible attacks. Mental imagery and fluidity has allowed the introduction and use of weapons in kata like Jutte, which I encourage within my Dojo. To perform Jutte with a staff (Jo), for example, has helped students to produce many mental pictures i.e. variations of an individual movement, which expands to each step of the kata. These images have helped to develop feeling, focus and posture whist passing through Kime, for with a weapon one learns to pass through, not stop at a target.

Kata, Kihon and indeed partner work can now advance beyond step, punch, block, and kick. Throws, armlocks, wrist and elbow locks, avoidance, escapes and atemi strikes can all be practiced to produce the Jitsu aspect of practice, but maintaining to Do essence. Kendo, Iaido and Aikido brought yet another concept to my practice. Defence from (Suwari Geiko) sitting position. In fact many defences in these arts began from these postures. The first point, I found was that power was increased in the hips and legs. Practice from this position, I now believe, is necessary to develop strength and suppleness. Pushing from the hips is necessary to move from this position and the feeling can then be transferred to standing. To lean forwards with the head and shoulders would be extremely bad for ones looks (and ones health), when defending from a kick, for example. If tension is used the body cannot flow smoothly and ones defence would be beaten by a bigger opponent. Body movement and rotation, in order to deflect blows is invaluable (like a sword would parry and cut).

Imagine age uke from kneeling. The power decending onto it would certainly bring your opponent down on you, but if you arc the arm to join the line of attack and rotate the body off his kime point, his balance and posture would be destroyed, and your counter with the rotation would be final.

Spin and counter using the body weight, moving off attackers kime point. Continue the direction of his attack to break his posture.

When standing, this avoidance movement breaks down into Irimi and tenkan. The first side step is past the attack. The second rotates through one hundred and eighty degrees to produce a deflecting action and avoid a blow penetrating deep into ones surface. Irimi is easy to explain as we perform it in daily life. Imagine having a bag of shopping and you are in a busy shopping centre or mall. As a person approaches you, you lead with the left hand and leg, brushing past the other person on an angle. You step beyond the body area and then step through with the rear arm, hip and leg to continue on your course. This is Irimi, and is done without thought. You are very close, but avoid contact, this is ideal. If attacked, you could turn and twist to miss being struck, yet be on top of your opponent to apply a pressure point, or an atemi strike. (this could be the first move of any kata, and down the middle of most). You will find that in practice, because one is conscious of an attack there is a tendency to jump or overstep sideways. One has now created negative direction and created a space between two bodies, which can act as a positive force for the attacker, who now has distance to use a kick, punch or back fist strike.

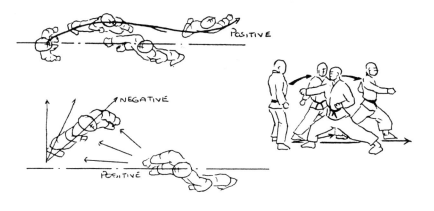

Fluidity and timing with minimum space to avoid and control the attacker

Tenkan begins with the same left leg (when attacked by the opponent's right) moves outside the attack. In this instance the body rotates to the left into, or rather through, kiba dachi. At the point where the chest is square to the opponent (one is now in kiba dachi at his side) the rear hip rotates taking the body backwards into a secondary kiba dachi. The body has rotated through one hundred and eighty degrees along the same line past the side of the attacker. Providing the movement has passed the back of the attacking arm, then his secondary technique will be limited. He must turn to the rear to attack again.

During this process one can counter with a leg sweep, stamping kick to the side or back of the knee, kidney, floating rib, side of the neck, base of the skull and all nerve points in these areas.

If stepping inside the arm beware of walking onto the opponents retracted fist. This can be overcome by striking with the first hip rotation. The whole of the right side is being driven through a curve to deliver an empi, taisho, koken, shuto and haito with full entrance of the body.

Fig 1) outside avoidance joining the circle (Tenkan)

A, B & C are maximum hip entrance points where strikes can be driven in.

Fig 2) Inside entrance

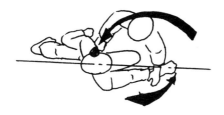

Hips spiral down and forwards into kime.

Exhale and strike in one single movement.

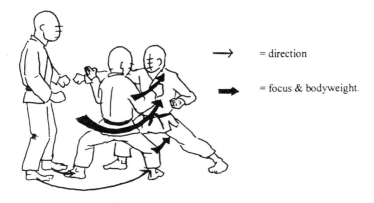

⟶   = direction

⟹   = focus & bodyweight.

Now with these principals and ideas understood, we can proceed to apply
them in the series of kata that follow.

Taikyoku Shodan (first Cause 1)

N

W —— E

S

Pattern shape

① Yoi Dachi
Turn head E

② drop hips to
front stance
Gedan barai

③ push through right
front stance
oi tsuki chudan

⑤ Push through left
Front stance
Oi tsuki chudan

④ turn W &
deliver gedan barai

bring weight over
left leg
R leg sweeps 180 W

Weight over R leg
Left leg sweeps 90 .S.

⑥ left gedan barai, in zenkutsu. S.

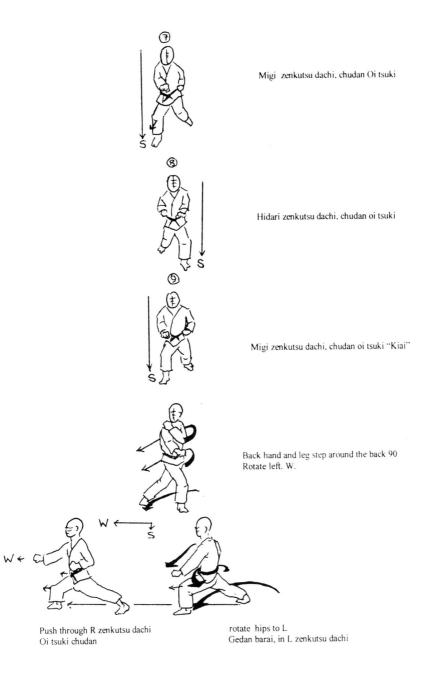

Migi zenkutsu dachi, chudan Oi tsuki

Hidari zenkutsu dachi, chudan oi tsuki

Migi zenkutsu dachi, chudan oi tsuki "Kiai"

Back hand and leg step around the back 90
Rotate left. W.

Push through R zenkutsu dachi
Oi tsuki chudan

rotate hips to L
Gedan barai, in L zenkutsu dachi

Rotate hips to left gedan barai, left zenkutsu dachi

push through R front stance & oi tsuki chudan

back hand and back leg stepping around the rear & rotate 90 to L

⑱

⑲

E

⑰

Right front stance with Chudan oi tsuki

N

⑯

Left front stance with Chudan oi tsuki

⑮

Right front stance with Chudan oi tsuki

N

⑭

⑫

⑬

Left zenkutsu dachi & Left gedan barai. N

E

Bring weight over L leg R leg sweeps 180 degrees

rotate E & deliver gedan barai

push through left front stance with oi tsuki chudan

Push through L front
Stance & oi tsuki chudan
sweep

turn left W &
deliver gedan barai

bring weight over
left leg. Right

through 180 degrees

"Yamae"
pull back knee to draw left hip
back, rotating 90 degrees from W to S.

Taikyoku Nidan (first Cause 2)

This kata is identical in form and posture as the previous kata, except that
the three flowing punches from north to south are changed to jodan oi
tsuki. Since the third punch is at jodan, on stepping around the back at
ninety degrees, the last punch will sweep down to gedan to cover, until
the left hand can deliver gedan barai. With a feeling of Ki this sweeping
hand may also hook behind the head to bring the opponent into a throw
like tae otoshi. It is this specific movement that is the focus of our
imagination, in this kata.

Taikyoku Sandan (First cause 3)

From Yoi dachi (hachi dachi/ ready stance), the sequence of movements and pattern of direction are similar to the previous two kata. When turning to the East or West however the back stance used, before the step and punch. Cross the hands, as if to deliver a Juji uke (cross block), or a ude uke (outer block). The left hand in front when stepping to the left. Right hand in front when stepping to the right.

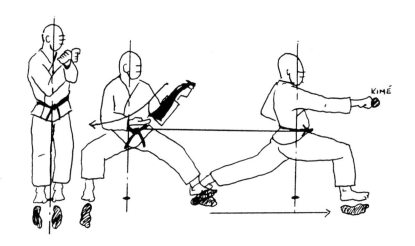

The centre line is the same as Taikyoku, so the punches are back to chudan, as with the east and West.

Remember therefor that after the third punch and the Kiai, one should turn, with a 90-degree step across the back to produce a back stance with a middle level outward block. The left hand will be in front when crossed, as one will rotate the hips to achieve the rotation to step, but also to deliver the power for the block.

Taikyoku Yodan (First cause 4)

N
W —|— E
S

kiai
pattern
Shape
kiai

Yoi dachi

turn E with left cat stance
& right Jodan taisho (palm)

slide left leg out
& left age uke

push through into R
front stance & oi tsuki

Push through left
front stance &

slide right leg out
& right age uke

turn W into right cat stance
and left jodan taisho (palm)

bring weight over L
leg as right leg sweeps
180 degrees

Weight over right leg
left leg sweeps 90 degrees to .S.

left age uke, zenkutsu dachi. S.

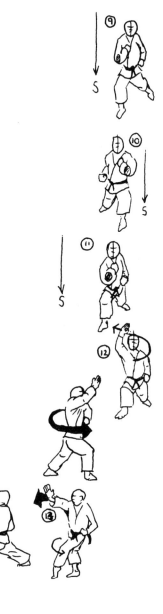

9) Right chudan empi uchi
   right zenkutsu dachi

10) Left chudan empi uchi
    left zenkutsu dachi

11) Right chudan empi uchi
    right zenkutsu dachi &
    "Kiai"

12) Do not step, but arc right
    hand from empi out into
    jodan shuto uchi
    (knife hand strike).

Back leg steps round 90 degrees
into L neko ashi dachi,
L. elbow rotates to strike, E &
R taisho rotates to jodan

13) Push taisho,R. whilst in
    left stance, left chudan empi

14) Pull back taisho to hip & L hand
    to jodan age uke, slide into L
    zenkutsu dachi

15) Push through R front stance &
    punch oi tsuki chudan

Do not step, but arc right hand from empi using the joint has a hinge & strike jodan shuto uchi. 23)

Right empi uchi chudan right zenkutsu dachi. 22)

Left empi uchi chudan left zenkutsu dachi. 21)

Right empi uchi chudan right zenkutsu dachi. 20)

Left zenkutsu & left age uke from empi. 19)

16) Rotate R & push taisho L in right cat stance, right chudan empi

17) pull back taisho to hip R hand to jodan age uke

18) push through L front stance & oi tsuki chudan

67

Back leg steps round 90 degrees
E. left elbow rotates to strike empi
To W. R taisho rotates to jodan

pass through cat stance into L
  zenkutsu dachi, age uke

push through R
zenkutsu R oi tsuki

Turn head W,
push left hand W

Push forward into L
Zenkutsu dachi, oi
Tsuki

slide out into zenkutsu dachi
right age uke & left ushiro
empi

turn into R
into cat stance
left jodan taisho

bring weight over L
rotate 180 degrees

"Yamae" pull back the right knee, pulling the body weight back over it. Rotating simultaneously

through 90 degrees from the West to face South. Finish in hachi dachi (natural stance).

1 Heine Shodan (Peaceful mind)

From the basic technique sections, the diagram and direction taken from the Taikyoku kata, forms and rotation etc can be deduced. Therefore the following Kata will concentrate, not on the scientific breakdown, but rather the practical applications, to help develop mental pictures and thus produces more feeling (remember there are many variations). The following are shown to give a practical insight, whilst still maintaining the science of the movement.

Ready posture

1) movement, posture & technique block to
2) break his momentum turning it into negative force

3)   = centre of gravity moves
      forward to give stability as it moves
      downwards through the technique.

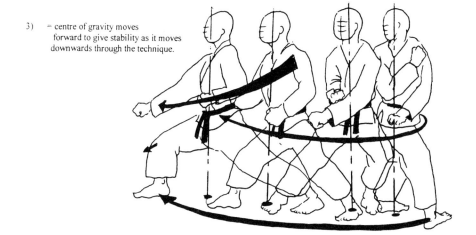

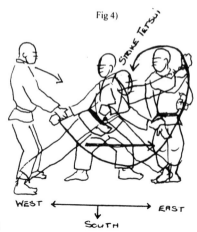
Fig 4)

Pulling with the back knee, and keeping ones posture upright, rotate the grabbed wrist, so that the little finger leads back, and to the rear foot (do not bend the arm as this encourages strength). The weight of the body drop, the pulling hand and a rotation of the wrist produces 1) a release Of grip or 2) breaking of the opponents posture. By pulling back the front leg at the same time the hips can start to rotate, so that a step through is possible and a punch can be delivered from the other side of the body (through to the W). After the step and punch turn to the S with left gedan barai, in zenkutsu dachi. Assume your attack has been grabbed (at the wrist), and repeat the escape we have just covered in Fig 4, up to age uke. Step through with age Uke (with a feeling of Uchi), so you step through striking the opponents arm. At the same time pull back the arm that is being held to a) break free or b) dislocate their elbow joint.

a)   b)

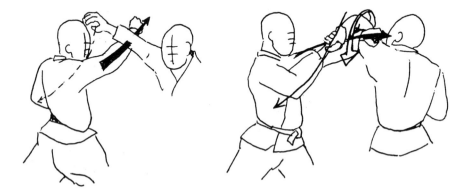

Age uke is performed in zenkutsu dachi, three times after the initial
escape facing S. The third age uke should finish on the right arm and leg.
From this point the kata resumes the pattern and sequence of
taikyoku shodan right through to the third oi tsuki N (right arm and leg).
From this point, whilst turning and moving E and then W, the flowing
movement of the hips and the centre of gravity is prominent.

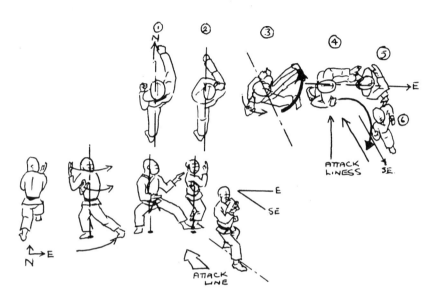

As the weight and centre of gravity are brought over the front (right) leg,
it produces a balanced rotation and left leg sweep. Then on completion of
the turn, a small forward transfer (forward now being to the E) provides
the momentum behind the shuto, to ensure a positive action and so
prevent a leaning back posture. At this point, ones feeling should be of a
threat from the right (i.e. coming from the S or SE).
Ones weight and therefore body is over the rear of your stance, so by
moving up to and passing beyond the front leg you avoid opponents focus
point by half the width of a body.

One is now poised to move diagonally, using shuto uke or uchi to the attacking arm, having covered

You're own ribs with the left hand.

Never be at the end of your opponent's kime point.

Heine shodan demonstrates one method of achieving this through body movement.

The combination of movements to the E is repeated to the W completing the kata to the S.W. Yamaewill draw back the left leg to hachi dachi facing S

Heine Nidan

The first steps to multi-directional simultaneous defence and counters.
From ready stance the first movement incorporates to jodan (upper level),
in the form of age uke and Haishu, moving an opponent whom has double
grabbed ones wrists. He is projected off balance (east) to put him on the
line of a secondary attacker, or defending two strikes from the front
(south) and the side (east).
Again we see the body weight moving into the attacker from the east. It
should be noted that in many cases, moving into the attack could reduce
the risk of injury, as you have moved off the opponents focus point.
Contact, if you remained on line, would be made at the early part
of the attack. Hip entrance would not be complete, the twist of the wrist,
or the lock of a thrusting leg would not be achieved, balance and posture
would be broken.

Fig 1	fig 2

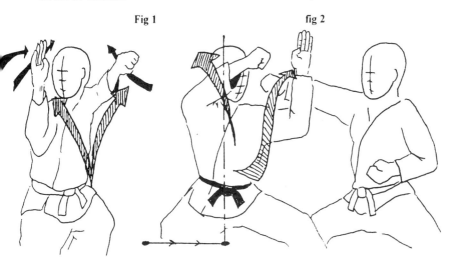

Fig 2 shows the first body movement of the kata. The body weight is
moving down and into the attack.
A lowering and advancing of the centre of gravity (at the tanden point).

From this strong posture the arms can pull apart with the elbows. The arms open into a double block, or two back fist strikes (fig 3)

(fig 3)

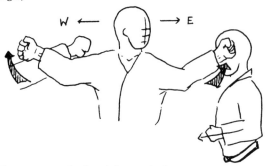

If we assume the hand forward of the face is east. Then one can **(fig 4)** pull it back to grab or parry. At the same time the rear hand sweeps forward to punch (the weight of the opponent falling forward). The power sweeps in from the west. Penetration of the punch is Increased by the rotation to an inverted hand position. (fig 4). The body weight is driven forwards ,by pushing the hips forwards, thrusting into front stance to close the distance, so that the low-level block can punch through the groin

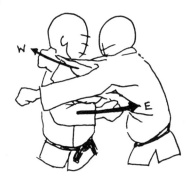

(fig 5)

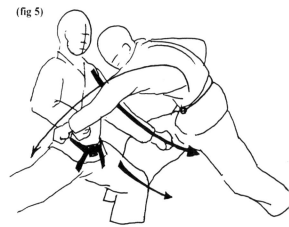

Movements 2, 3, 4 & 5 are repeated to the right (west) to the point of the gedan strike (decide if you are taking the first opponent from the east with you into the second coming from the west?). Now an attack is delivered from the right (north). Draw the back leg, half way up to the front knee, up into mae geri position (the knee being high to the chest). The hands are drawn back to the left hip. Looking to the right (north), execute a yoko geri keage, and a uraken strike (jodan). The kick could in effect strike the ribs, rise up under the arm/elbow joint, or strike under the jaw (fig 6)

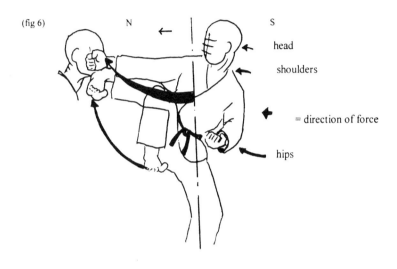

(fig 6)   N   S

head

shoulders

= direction of force

hips

In some schools the uraken is used to circle in and strike an arm, whilst the leg locks straight to strike the face. Fig 6B shows why this variation does not run with the general principals of this conveyed in this book. Control and balance, combined with positive body movement should be the aim. Fig 6B shows a contradiction to this by producing a negative force effect.

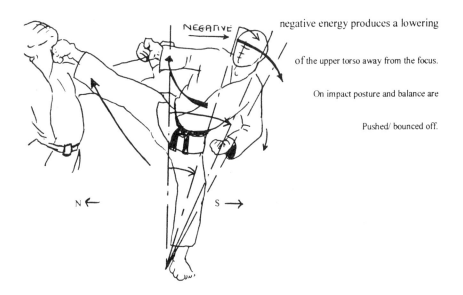

NEGATIVE

negative energy produces a lowering

of the upper torso away from the focus.

On impact posture and balance are

Pushed/ bounced off.

N ←   S →

The next movement is to draw back the kick, keeping the knee high and stepping or stamping down (north) onto the opponent's hip, knee or shin until back stance is achieved. After the yoko geri, pull
back the uraken to cover the ribs at the rear (south). Bring the opposite hand up to the face. After the stamp, in back stance, strike with shuto uke (left hand)

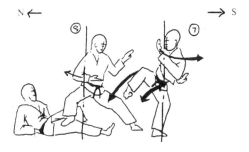

N ←   → S

Step 9 is to slide through with the right foot into back stance with a shuto uke (or uchi) depending on your visualisation of its application. Step through into another back stance and repeat the hand
technique. After the third step and shuto, one assumes the opponent counters with gyaku tsuki chudan. Step 11 is to use the shuto arm (L.) to press down onto the oncoming strike. Here the arm can
go down and forward (Irimi), down and back to accept and re-direct (tenkan), or straight down. However a simple arm movement will not always be enough. In fact it would take the punch from the
chest into the groin. The use of the hand only, would also leave the attacker on posture. We overcome these problems with body movement co-ordinated with the arm. As the pressing block (osai uke) swings down, and say pushes forward, the hips drop too. The result is a total re-direction of your opponents' techniques (and following body mass), assuming the punch is meant.

Fig 10   ———→ S

Fig 11

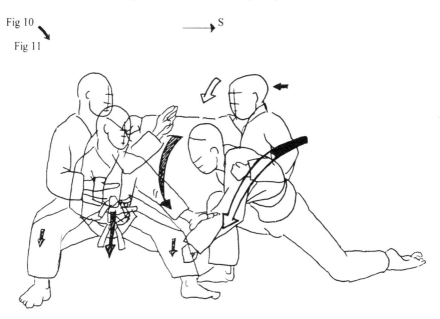

Step through right zenkutsu and deliver a right nukite over the pressing arm, the latter now acting as a shock absorber against any attack to the R elbow joint as one kiai's.

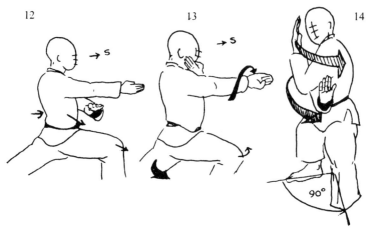

After the spear hand, consider being grabbed at the right wrist. Rotate anti clockwise to break the grip and commence a feeling of projection through the fingers, whilst bringing the L hand over for shuto fig 13. Turn to face W into back stance with shuto. Consider, did you bring the wrist grabbing opponent with you as you turn, or did you force him to release? (also at this mid point of the kata the movements W and E are identical to the end of heine shodan). Recall that after four directional shuto in back stance one will finish in L back stance (having avoided strikes by moving in to the front leg and stepping out at an angle). At this move 17 one should be facing NE.

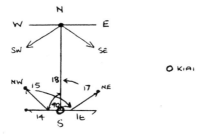

At this point bring up the R arm, so that both arms are crossed, with the R hand driving up forwards across the body, so providing a strong cover ready for the next posture change.

Step with the nearest front leg (45 degrees to the N) to face the oncoming attack. Pass through kokutsu into zenkutsu dachi, flowing and driving the R hip forwards (note; the left leg forwards, right hip forwards). This alters the direction from sideways to forwards, thus producing the force to make the gyaku ude uke effective (fig 18).
Using the momentum of the hips, bring the centre of gravity over the L leg. the weight can then be taken off the R leg, so that it can be lifted to deliver a front kick (keage), snapping into the groin to stun the opponent (fig 19).

(fig 18)   (fig 19)

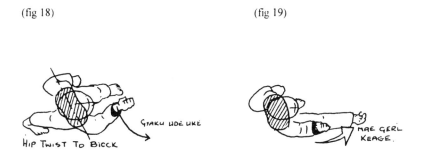

Place the kicking leg onto the floor, through cat stance and sliding forward. Ones R leg is now to the front, but the L hip is rotated forwards to launch a reverse punch (gyaku - tsuki), flowing from the hip into the elbow and along the fore arm, rotating through the wrist and out of the fist.
Pull the L elbow in towards the centre line, in order that the fist is brought in with it (feeling of the little finger pulling underneath towards ones centre line L to R). After passing the centre line, snap the arm back out to the gyaku ude uke position, rotating the thumb over and forwards R to L (fig 20).

(fig 20)

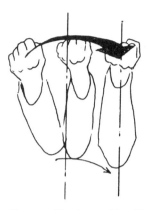

Centre of body   side of body

Body weight travels forwards over the R leg. Weight can be taken off the L leg, so that mae geri keage can be used again.

Slide forwards with the L leg into front stance, driving the R hip (opposite hip) forwards, pushing the force into the R reverse punch.

One draws back the R elbow across the centre of the body and supports it with the L fist. Drive both the L fist and R arm forwards, as the R side of the body lunges through. The front stance and the supported block (morote uke) focusing through the opponent and breaking his posture (at the end of the line N).

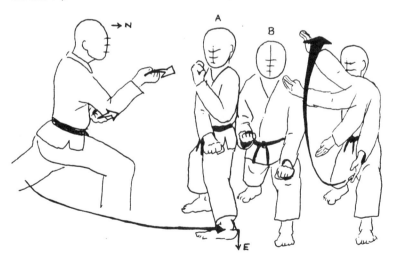

Rotate the left hip and leg around to produce a sweeping action (leading with the heel). The left moves up to the shoulder, preparing to deliver gedan barai/ uchi. The right rotating and sweeping around to gedan (as in A). this parry's or covers the body until the body weight is dropped forward to the east, providing hip entrance behind the left gedan (as in B). Assuming the gedan wrist is grabbed, open the hand and rotate the little finger back towards the body. This principal is to relax and break free, or pull the opponents' arm down and towards the body, continuing in a circle up to jodan. (If ones arm bends during this process, strength and tension will result and the upper torso will feel rigid). At jodan the arm bends and pushes forwards, delivering an age uke.
This push and rotation of the wrist would
then bend the opponents arm at the elbow
and wrist.
Note; when pulling back up to age uke
pull the posture from front to back stance,
and back into front with the twist.

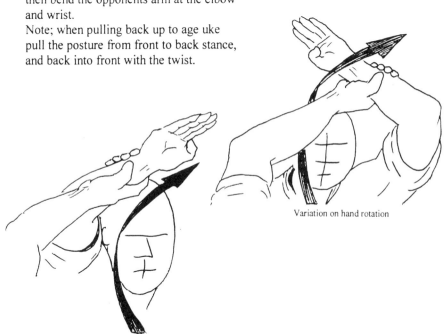

Variation on hand rotation

From stance (L zenkutsu dachi) facing E, the upper body is now facing forty-five degrees i.e. S.E with the left arm raised to age uke. From here the feeling and the step with the R side travels S.E into R zenkutsu dachi and the R arm delivers age uke/ uchi. As the L pulls back (still held by the opponent). The block, leading with the fist would snap or dislocate the opponents arm.

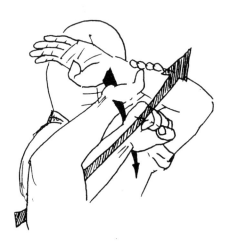

Rotate from the S.E to W with gedan barai and repeat the escape, step and break. On the second breaking point (the last move of the kata), "Kiai".

Heine Sandan

W   N   E

S

In basic form, from yoi dachi, cross the hands in front of the chest (L in front of R). Rotate L to the east into back stance and middle level outer block. Since the attack is coming from the side, as we advance it is weak to bring up the hands at ninety degrees (the ribs are exposed). If the left arm were pushed against (A), a block would be impossible.

From yoi, rotate the upper body forty-five degrees left with the arms crossing in front of the chest i.e. S.E. This puts the fists ahead of the elbows, giving a positive directional feeling as in fig (B).

Fig (A) weak & negative   fig (B) strong & positive

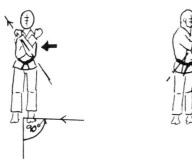

Rotate L and move through neko ashi dachi (cat foot stance) into kokutsu (back stance) and snap the ude uke across, striking the forearm, bicep, shoulder (depending on entrance). Pulling the weight centre over the front leg, so the feet are together, centre of gravity over the knees and ankles. Block ude uke (R), gedan barai (L), as a simultaneous defence (or attack?). Repeat the movement ude uke (L) and gedan barai (R). All can be strikes or blocks, or a mental combination can be felt at any stage (i.e. a double block, a double strike, a block and a strike).

Leg sweep one hundred and eighty degrees right (W) into back stance and repeat the whole process.

Move left ninety degrees (S) with back stance, morote uke (do not allow the fist to come behind the elbow). Since the R hand is pushing behind the elbow, it would be greatly restricted in the defensive format. Logic uses the extended, and better-located L arm to combat the next attack. Osai uke is again used, and in order to maximise penetration the body weight drops, as in heine nidan. In fact the heine nidan sequence continues with R step into front stance with nukite.

Aikido covers, in depth, the use of body movement against grabs or attempted grabs. Part of this philosophy now comes into play. Assuming the spear hand has been grabbed. Human reaction is tension or strength, in a desperate need to break free. But the kata at this point shows total acceptance.

Allow the whole R arm to go limp (relaxed) and move forwards towards your aggressor, by rotating the L hip one hundred and eighty degrees from the rear with a backward spin, so that your trapped arm is wrapped around ones own back. The body position finishes in kiba dachi (horse riding), side facing and the momentum of the rotation snaps gedan barai/ uchi into the aggressors inside leg. Or if the standard momentum (as previously described) is driven forwards, the groin or lower abdomen may be struck.

Kata provides a solution to each situation, but it is always important to look at your position, your options, your targets and your weaknesses to provide an overall assessment of effort and force required to escape. Of course as a group practice the visual perception must look standardised and regimented.

Ones R leg is at the rear now, and the left hip has rotated forwards we now complete the flow by driving the R side forwards into front stance punching R oi tsuki with a strong "kiai".

At one school in particular, it was emphasised that it was always a punch to the solar plexus. But let us consider what happens next. The punching fist rotates clockwise and drives vertically upwards. The back leg is drawn to the front and the body is rotated one hundred and eighty degrees to face N, so that you are facing back to the original starting point. Is this a punch driven up under the jaw as you move up to your opponent, your back turning to him as you prepare to take on another challenger? Yes, perhaps but let us consider a more adventurous vision and application. On the last punch (S) strike through the floating ribs driving it between the ribs and the left arm. As the arm drives up it passes behind the shoulder, so as you rotate a hip throw could be used. As the arm passes vertical and comes down towards your hip it traps the opponents arm against the back of your neck. As you continue the arc his body weight is driven down and an arm or shoulder lock is applied.

Since the first movement N is a mikazuki geri (crescent kick) with the R leg the knee will strike the face of your unfortunate aggressor. The crescent kick is delivered and you land in kiba dachi. If your opponent is still trapped he will be thrown over your leg (although he would have been struck by the oncoming attack); you have used him as a shield. If thrown prior to an attack, your mikazuki geri would have served to step over him in the process of intercepting a second opponent.

We see then that many things are occurring within this kata, avoiding, trapping, throwing and body movement to bring one opponent between you and others (to do this in group fight could create a Breathing space).

Mikazuki geri is performed three times (in a right, left, right sequence). Each time finishing in kiba dachi (usually in a stamping manner). The fists on the hips, elbows rotate to block an attack to your chest.

	4	3	2	I
	return to hip	hikate & uraken	empi uke	mikazuki geri

If the elbow is trapped, as at 2), pull the arm back to the hip to create space then strike out uraken and return to the hip. After repeating the sequence three times you should finish travelling north in a R kiba dachi, as at 4). Push out the R hand (north) to strike taisho (perhaps trapping or blocking). Rotate the R foot and pull from kiba dachi, through kokutsu dachi and on into zenkutsu dachi, delivering hidari (left) chudan oi tsuki.

Here at the end of the north line we encounter an interesting series of movements. Draw up the right leg to the left and assume a short kiba dachi. Assuming that your opponent is at the end of this N line, it would appear that you are offering a free shot to your groin. Could this move be right?

If you push out taisho (previous), on the R leg kiba. Should your opponent step back (r leg), as you step through and punch with the left. Then as you bring up the R leg, you could, as you perform your short kiba dachi; actually attack the inside of his leg, breaking his posture by forcing his knee joint out to his left (E).

As you then bring your left leg around one hundred and eighty degrees to the east your right elbow would strike his floating ribs as it passes through to strike over the L shoulder. The left arm draws back to strike empi to the groin or chest. If the strike to the ribs was effective causing him to bend over, or go down onto one knee the empi could even be into his face.

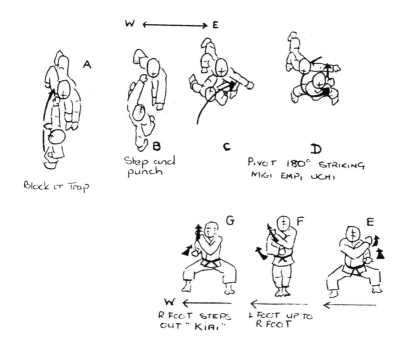

W ←———→ E

A

B
Step and
punch

C

D
Pivot 180° Striking
Migi Empi Uchi

Block or Trap

G

F

E

W ←
R Foot Steps
out " Kiai"

←
L Foot up to
R Foot

←

Heine Yodan (Peaceful Mind 4)

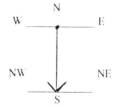

From yoi dachi (ready stance) the first movement is similar to heine nidan, except the hands open with a feeling of projection to the E. This could allow an escape from a double grab, as well as the conventional double block scenario. The R hand forcing a release of the opponents grip on your L hand as they cross and pull apart at the top, and opening of the technique. Push down through the heels and rotate one hundred and eighty degrees to repeat the series of actions to the W.

Bring both hands (clenched) back over the right shoulder step out with the left leg S into front stance, whilst performing a juji uke type block. The feeling should be of a gedan barai (or Uchi) with the left arm and a punch, possibly to the shin or fore arm, with the right.

Pulling with the left knee, slide through into a right kokutsu dachi covering or blocking morote uke. Drive the hips forwards, bringing the weight over the right leg. Raise the left knee and bring both hands back to right hikate. Perform yoko geri keage and uraken to the left (E). Make sure both strikes hit the same area of the opponent i.e. head/ face. Step down through neko ashi dachi (cat foot stance) and on into zenkutsu dachi. Bring the left hand through and behind the shoulder or head of your opponent.

Rotate the right hip and deliver a right gyaku mawashi empi uchi to hit your left hand (through the opponent).

Drive both hands down, returning both hands to left hikate (bringing the half-conscious assailant to his knees). Turn the left foot to the right (south) and bring the weight over the left leg.

This will move your body away from the next attack, as you raise the right leg and kick yoko geri and

strike uraken to the right (W). Bring the right hand behind the shoulder or
head, as to the E and repeat the step and elbow strike as you finish in
right zenkutsu dachi (W). Imagine a kick coming from your left side (S).
Block with gedan shuto uchi, whilst the right defends through jodan.
Pivot on the heels through one hundred and eighty degrees into left
zenkutsu, pulling the left hand back to draw a punch past the side of your
face, whilst bringing the right hand around, at shoulder level, to
Strike (S) shuto to the side of the neck Fig 1.

Fig 1   fig 2

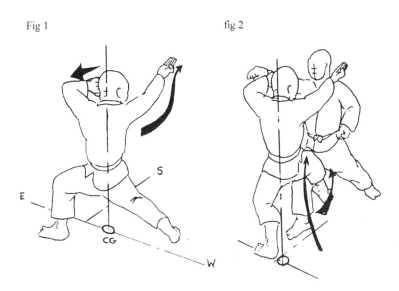

Fig 2, Bring weight forwards over the left knee to allow you to drive the
right knee up to the right (S) and deliver mae geri keage into the groin.
Pull back the right hand towards the left armpit, reaching over the top
with the left hand to grab the opponents hair, collar, shirt, tie etc. Grab the
opponent but do not pull (remember, he is on two feet and you are still
only on one). Step down, right foot forwards (S) into the opponent, still
holding with the left hand. Now the pull comes, bringing the left hand
back to the hip, striking with a right ude uke

to the chin, nose, chest, shoulder (joint or nerve). Bring up the back (L) leg behind the right. This allows the hips to flow forwards right up to the opponent fig a,b,c

a)   b)   c) "Kiai"   d)

N _____ S

Pull the hands in front of the stomach (right on top of left). Hands are open with the palms facing up. Step back N.W with the left leg, fig d. Rotate the left hip and knee, so that the weight is brought N.W into zenkutsu dachi and drive the crossed hands straight up and forwards to deliver an open handed juji uke to jodan fig e.

fig g   fig f   fig e

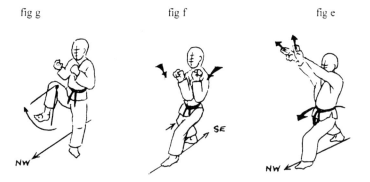

Pull back, fig f, (with grab or double block), using the weight moving backwards and downwards, to break posture. Again pull with the front knee, raise the back (right) leg to snap kick. The right foot steps down and slides forward, so that the right leg moves into zenkutsu dachi with a migi oi tsuki chudan (right lunge punch to the middle/ solar plexus). (Reminder; do not fall into a stance after a kick, if the opponents posture is positive. i.e. do not allow yourself to be open to kicks or foot sweeps). Passing through cat stance and sliding into posture, which also drives the hip behind the punch.

Rotate the hips, as in fig I, to bring the left hip forward and punch through with left gyaku tsuki

Fig H   Fig I

Pull back through cat stance, whilst drawing the hands across the stomach. The right leg passing across the N onto the N.E. line.
Push the right leg from cat foot stance to front stance with jodan juji uke (upper level cross block).
Follow the sequence from (e) figure, to kick, step oi tsuki, gyaku tsuki etc on the N.E line. After Completion of the last gyaku tsuki (left), in a right front stance, bring up the arms, ready to block morote uke. Keeping the hands forward of the elbow, step forty five degrees into a left back stance

Blocking across and forward. Repeat the morote uke in back stance two more times N.

From back stance, left morote uke, push your body weight forwards into front stance (this movement is designed to help you reach your opponent without risk to your own stability). At the same time, reach up to grab your opponents head, hair, ears, collar Fig J.

Fig J   Fig K

"Kiai"

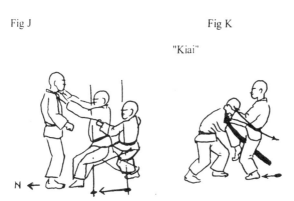

Fig K then shows the weight being brought forwards onto the left leg, allowing the hips to drive through and bring up the right knee (hiza geri). At the same time bring down the arms past the knee along with whatever they were holding and "Kiai". Keeping the right foot high, rotate the right hip to thrust fumikomi (stamping kick) to the hip, thigh or knee joint. Slide the edge of the foot down his shin and onto the top of his foot. Rotate the upper body one hundred and eighty degrees left (S) and land in back stance blocking or covering with shuto (S) and striking with a right empi (N) to the fallen opponents head.

Fig L   Fig M   Fig N

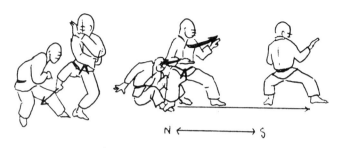

Pull with the left knee, pushing the right leg forward (N) into back stance
and shuto uke (or Uchi) to
finish (yamae).

Heine Godan (Peaceful mind five)

W ┬ E

S

In the early kata forms attention was to show the form and direction, so
that the pattern could be practiced fairly quickly. Once into the physical
performance, concentrated towards the feeling of fluidity and posture and
balance. An in depth, but open minded approach to the actual techniques
and variations of defence that are available, whether avoiding, blocking
or striking on straight lines or circular.
Now that the principals are being applied and understood (eventhough
they are only basic), control of breathing can be introduced. Naturally
this will stop you becoming breathless, and will help in feeling
the ki energy, which is to be projected through the body. The mind and
the body then become focused to maximise the "kime" at any single point
during your practice.

"Yoi" or ready, is the point of bringing your body, but also your mind to attention, or a preparatory state. Aware of your surroundings, of your opponent/s, of your complete circumstances and the acceptance of them. Begin by taking on breath for each technique, breathing out on the performance of each. The aim however, is to breath out through a series of techniques to help with the flow of them.

With this in mind we can begin.

1)   2)   3)

1) Glance and step left into hidari kokutsu dachi and deliver hidari ude uke. In the same breath
2) Rotate the right hip and drive through a gyaku tsuki chudan.
3) Taking a sharp breath in, looking over the left shoulder. Pull in the right leg, up to the left, so that you are moving away from an attack from your rear. Breathing out, rotate right, so that your feet come together facing S, (As is the whole body) and punch with the left hand across the body. Use the spin of the hips to draw back the right arm to strike empi N. (rear). In an advanced form you could also be stepping up to an opponent, and applying a arm bar or elbow dislocation, whilst bringing him around into the line of a secondary attacker.
4) Take in air sharply and exhale slowly as you step right (west) into kokutsu dachi and block / or strike ude uke/ uchi.

5) Rotate the left hip and strike with the left gyaku tsuki chudan.

6) Taking a sharp breath in, look ninety degrees to the left (S), pull in the left leg up to the right (moving away from a rear attack, or into the previous attack). Breath out and punch or lock and break, as the spin provides the power and downward spiral momentum.

7) Inhale, move forward (S) in kokutsu dachi, blocking morote uke (breath out slowly throughout)

8) During this breathing out, continue the weight of the body forwards into hidari zenkutsu dachi and block juji uke (or left gedan barai, right punch low level)

9) Inhale quickly and exhale as you open the hands and drive the cross block up to jodan, trapping an opponents punch

10) In the same breath rotate the hands and pull down to the right hip, applying a wrist lock, and pulling your attacker off balance towards you.

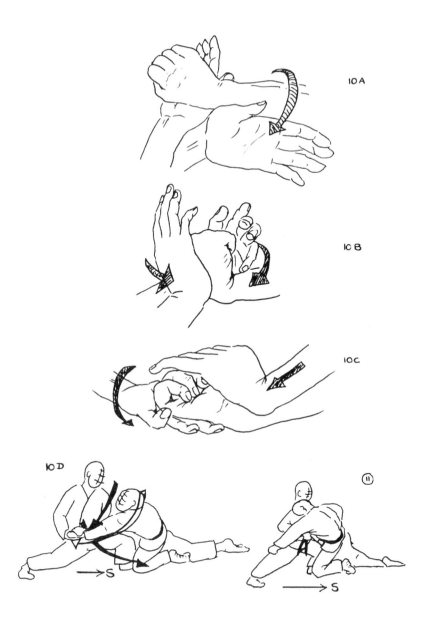

10 A

10 B

10 C

10 D

(11)

11) As the opponent falls forward, push forward with the hip and thrust the left arm forward into his groin or face. As the of the air is exhaled
12) Drive forwards into right zenkutsu dachi, oi tsuki and "kiai".

15   14   13   12

EXHALE

13) Rotate through left kokutsu dachi and exhale as
14) You continue to spin, bringing the right foot up to strike mikazuki geri chudan (crescent kick to middle).
15) Step down and slide into right kiba dachi and block gedan barai (complete your breath out through the kime point).
16) Breathe in, as you snap your head around to look (N). Exhale as your arms cross. The left hand pulls back and down to the right side. Your right hand extends to cover your face with taisho, pushing forward (S) and across.

EXHALE THROUGHOUT

17) Exhale and strike out, left shuto uchi to the shoulder joint, arm, neck or jaw
18) Inhale and pass the shuto hand behind the opponents' shoulders or head and exhale as the right foot sweeps up to strike the object your left hand is holding, using mikazuki geri (crescent kick).
19) Continue to breath out as you pull the right leg to chudan, rotate and strike mawashi empi to the same target.
20) Continue to exhale, or take a sharp intake of breath and start to exhale again. Step down (S) with the right leg. Bring the left leg up (behind the right) to the (S), striking morote uke

19   20   21

21) Rotate north stepping out with the left leg into Choji dachi (T stance), driving morote uke upwards. Used as a strike, covering action or as an escape from a grab around the shoulders. Breathing outwards here, to provide drive, feeling and or making the chest small to create space

22) Assuming the next attack is at your knees, either with a staff or a spinning leg sweep, it is important to leap high and avoid being struck. In training I have seen students bend knees, dropping the hips slightly, so that they could spring into the air. Unfortunately most were hit before they left the ground. Or they were "rapped" around the ankles after leaving the ground.

With practice, you can throw the right knee/ leg upwards to N. Provided the momentum is strong the body can be lifted high, pushing off the left leg, which lifts up behind the right, with the knees into the chest.

Fig22 through 23 incorporates a single exhale with spirit cry.

23   22

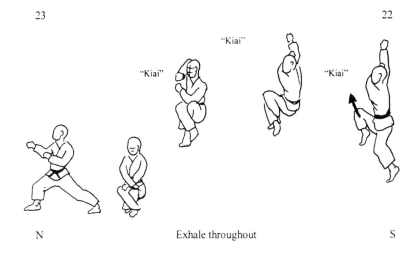

"Kiai"   "Kiai"   "Kiai"

N   Exhale throughout   S

To help fluidity and force through the Juji uke on landing, and into
23) The drive through with the R leg and R leading morote uke.

24) Having expelled all the air, the body automatically breathes in, turn 180 degrees S, breathe out slowly. Assume kokutsu dachi (left) with gedan barai over the knee. At the same time bring up the R hand high, the arm covering the R side of the head, driving vertically upwards. Fig 23

Fig 23 1   11   111

-- S
Exhale

11 Immediately move forward into front stance. Cover the face against a punch, whilst the R hand sweeps down to strike or grab the groin.
111 Twist and pull back, using the hips to get back into kokutsu dachi and gedan punch, R hand pulling back above the head.

Fig 24

Inhale, turn foot and bring body back, so that the two feet are together (thus performing a slow sweep)

N   Inhale---------------------------------- S

25 (Exhale) rotate the right side and move forwards into kokutsu dachi. R gedan barai (block or strike ?) and pull the left hand vertically upwards past the left side of the head (inhaling).

26) (Exhale) Push hips forwards into zenkutsu dachi covering the face and grab the groin again (possibly a second opponent?).

27) Again rock back into kokutsu dachi, R gedan barai and pull back with the left. Inhale whilst returning to ready stance (Hachi dachi).

-----------------X-----------------

The "Yin and the Yang" principal

Soft or hard, accept or reject. These ideas apply throughout the martial arts. Each provides principals that can bring an offensive situation to a conclusion.

Aikido moves around the direction of force, or joins with it to re-direct it, and so make the opponent off balance. To use this force against itself.

In kendo or jodo the weapon may parry or deflect the blow and cut or strike in an instant.

Karate, in all its forms, because of its thrusts and blows. Because of its straight lines and locking of joints and tensing of muscles e.g. at "kime", may seem in appearance to be the opposite extreme. To watch Goju Ryu, with its tense, slow practice, could on the surface appear static and hard? Applying the principals mentioned, and understanding and feeling the movement in kata, should be combined together to produce a greater range of options to any number of attacks. Flexibility of mind will provide a flexibility of defence, which can range from the basic block and counter strike. A hard rejection of your opponents advances. Or to move around an attack, circling in to accept the force and re-directing it into a spiral, bringing the body or force into yours, so that you take control of it. Bring it into a throw, into an armlock, into a choke, or any other close quarter technique.

Within the kata, when studied in depth and practiced slowly, with partners, these variations become apparent. Provided that your mind is not controlled by " Style limitations".

If we are to understand the saying " there is no first punch in Karate" then we must mentally produce the image to help us make sense of this.

Working from the basic principals of fighting, then surely someone has to lash out, or at least enter our space?

What of the idea that the defender is so relaxed, so fluid and so aware of his opponents feelings, that in the same breath as the strike, comes the defence (regardless of what the defence is, block, or counter strike).

Your body should move when your opponent's body moves. Two halves of a circle, which are brought together to make a single movement. Whether one side of the circle is soft and the other hard, or either soft, or both hard becomes irrelevant. The movement will be completed as one, with no beginning and no end. i.e. no first punch, no following counter. To move and then to strike, to block and then punch is a novice or "broken" form. The essence of defence, through concentration and focus, is to produce a conclusion, or combination of movements in one.

Two people, two movements, but a single kime. Let's assume you are against a wall, and are under threat. At the point your attacker lunges at you, step forward and rotate. He leads R, you step R.

You cover but allow the punch to continue on its path (but pull it gently and push it with your leading arm). Your bodies would revolve. You facing the wall, your attacker now is against it. A full circle is achieved in a single movement.

Let us now look at the soft and hard, the reject, or the accept, performed as part of a single action.

"Rejection is hard".

Opponent attacks R chudan oi tsuki
Defender rotates to drive the hip and fist towards the attacker (solar plexus, face, groin) to complete the fight.

Opponent attacks R chudan oi tsuki
Defender turns head away, lowering the body to avoid the strike. Drive the body weight towards the attacker. Rotating the hips, drive the kick ushiro geri or yoko geri, so that his momentum is halted, or re-directed to finish the fight.

Opponent strikes R chudan oi tsuki
Defender steps forward on the outside and strikes gyaku tsuki, nukite, taisho, and koken. Either over or under the arm, depending on height.

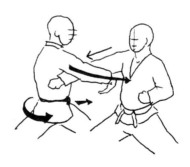

Opponent strikes R oi tsuki chudan
Defender steps L on the outside and rotates the hip with L uchi komi
(inner winding block). Trapping with the R arm and producing pressure
through the joint creating a negative force towards

 "A"

Opponent attacks R oi tsuki
Defender moves forwards to lunge shuto into the shoulder joint (or bicep,
or jaw), to re-direct his positive force, and turn it to negative force

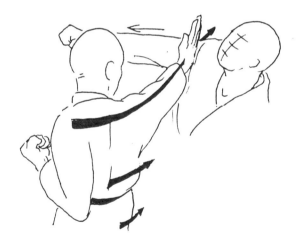

All your force is positive and hinged, from the left shoulder forwards
through the right arm.

Opponent punches R oi tsuki chudan.
Defender moves in with the R side, whilst rotating the upper body, and so too the arms, to parry or strike. By keeping the weight over the rear leg as the body turns, a kick may be incorporated into the movement. Using the spin and the dropping (or spiralling down), to provide the force/ power.

Even with these few examples, we can see that by moving with the opponent, with entrance, we can develop a drive through the line of attack, penetrating through or against the flow of force.

Accepting the attack, "Going with the flow."
Assuming positive force is travelling towards you, then negative force is that which travels away from you.
Here we do not intercept or oppose the positive force, but deflect, redirect or allow it to go past, or around us. Assume yourself to be the centre of a spinning universe. Bring the positive force around you, or spiral it into you, so that it becomes part of YOUR force, which you can control and direct.

Opponent strikes R oi tsuki (level irrelevant).
The defender moves off the line of attack, rotating and stepping to the right. One can cover the punch with a sweep of the left hand, whilst the R hand sweeps around the opponents head, (striking if necessary). With the rotation and joining of the circle you can bring his force around you until his posture is broken and his force is redirected towards the floor. You have avoided, struck and thrown tae otoshi, all in one action.

Opponent strikes R punch.
Defend by stepping in with the left, moving outside of the punching arm. Bring your leading L arm over his punch. Bringing your L side into his elbow or shoulder, re directing weight down into the floor.

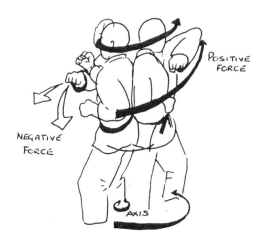

Opponent strikes R oi tsuki.
Defend by stepping and rotating on the R, whilst covering the punch.
Pivot on the R foot and bring the L hip around (rear). Bring the left elbow
up and around with the hip and deliver a ushiro empi uchi (jodan?).

Both the soft and hard, entering and accepting and the direct and circular,
are mere examples taken from a vast range of techniques. From more
basic karate, and jujitsu types, into an almost pure aikido form. The aim
here is not to teach the technique. It is rather an opening up of attitude,
where ideology and practice can be developed. This can break down and
overcome the "best style" syndrome and find an effective defensive way
"Do", without the mental confines imposed by "closed shop" attitudes
and tunnel vision associated with any single system.

Kata Patterns (Heine Sandan)

6 + 5   4   1   2+3

7
marte uke

8
OSAI UKE

9
NUKITE

10
GEDAN BARAI
KIBA DACHI

12   "KIAI"   11.
CHUDAN OI TSUKI

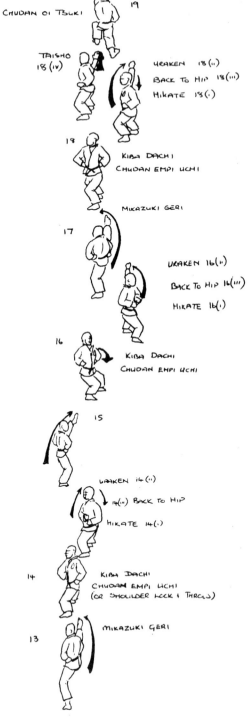

CHUDAN OI TSUKI

19

TAISHO
18 (IV)

URAKEN 18 (II)

BACK TO HIP 18 (III)

HIKATE 18 (I)

18

KIBA DACHI
CHUDAN EMPI UCHI

MIKAZUKI GERI

17

URAKEN 16 (II)

BACK TO HIP 16 (III)

HIKATE 16 (I)

16

KIBA DACHI
CHUDAN EMPI UCHI

15

URAKEN 14 (II)

14 (III) BACK TO HIP

HIKATE 14 (I)

14

KIBA DACHI
CHUDAN EMPI UCHI
(OR SHOULDER LOCK & THROW)

MIKAZUKI GERI

13

HEINE YODAN

JUJI UKE

MOROTE UKE

URAKEN

YOKO GERI KEAGE

GYAKU EMPI UCHI (MAWASHI)

URAKEN

YOKO GERI KEAGE

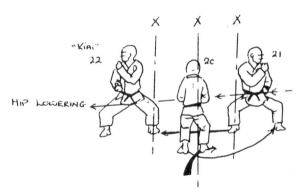

ROTATION AND "YORI ASHI" THROUGH AXIS POINT (X).

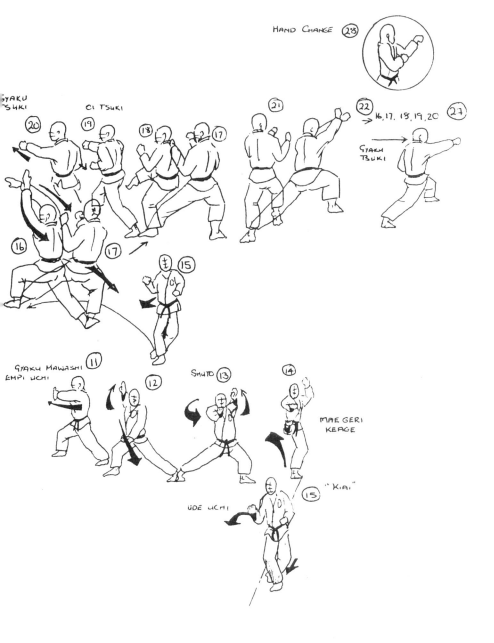

HAND CHANGE ㉘

GYAKU TSUKI ⑳   OI TSUKI ⑲   ⑱   ⑰   ㉑   ㉒ →16, 17, 18, 19, 20 ㉗

GYAKU TSUKI

⑯   ⑰   ⑮

GYAKU MAWASHI EMPI UCHI ⑪   ⑫   SHUTO ⑬   ⑭

MAE GERI KEAGE

UDE UCHI   ⑮   "KIAI"

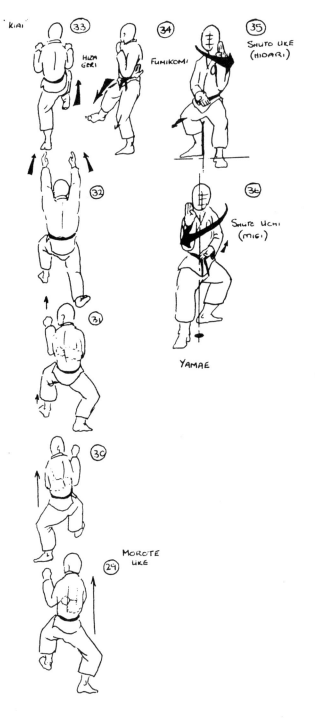

'KIAI

(33)

HIZA
GERI

(34)

FUMIKOMI

(35)

SHUTO UKE
(HIDARI)

(32)

(36)

SHUTO UCHI
(MIGI)

YAMAE

(31)

(30)

MOROTE
UKE

(29)

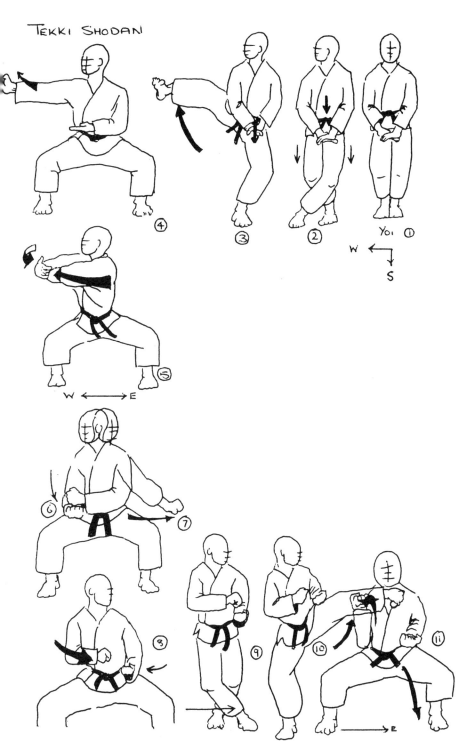

TEKKI SHODAN

④

③ ② Yoı ①

W ←
  ↓
  S

⑤

W ←——→ E

⑥ ⑦

⑧ ⑨ ⑩ ⑪

——→ E

115

"KIAI"

36
YAMAE

35

31 30 29 32 33 34

⑤ ④ ③ ② ①

⑨ ⑧ ⑦ ⑥

⑩ ⑪ ⑫ ⑬ ⑭ ⑮

Application of Nikkyo

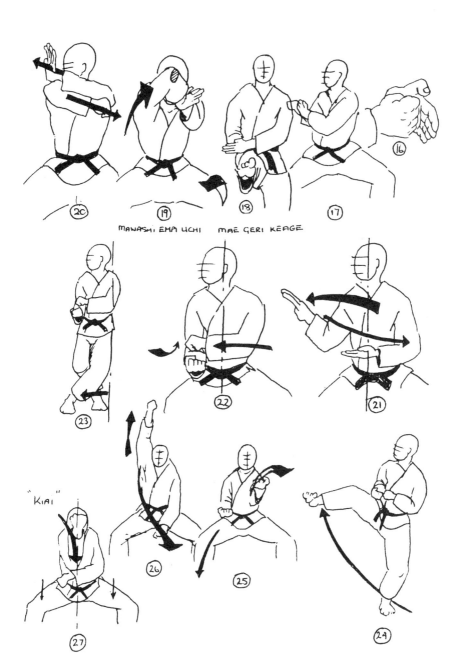

MAWASHI EMPI UCHI   MAE GERI KEAGE

"KIAI"

28 29 30

MAE GERI KEAGE
(HIDARI)

31 32

33 34 35 36

37 38 39 "KIAI"

40
"YAMAE"

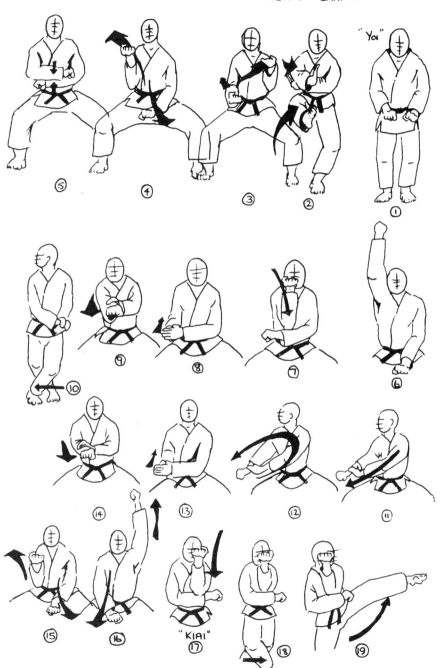

"Ya"

⑤ ④ ③ ② ①

⑩ ⑨ ⑧ ⑦ ⑥

⑭ ⑬ ⑫ ⑪

⑮ ⑯ "KIAI" ⑰ ⑱ ⑲

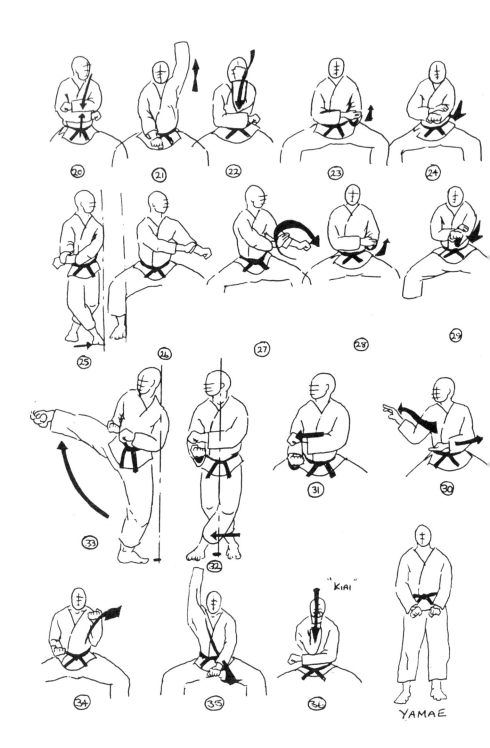

"KIAI"

YAMAE

Bassai Dai

"To Penetrate a Fortress"

W ——— E

SW

S

① ②

③ ④ ⑤

⑩ ⑨ ⑧ ⑦ ⑥

≥ND THROW   LIFT USING THE THIGH MUSCLES   To SCOOP A KICK

⑪   ⑫   ⑬   ⑭   ⑯   ⑮

₂ ⁼ KATE   SHUTO

DOUBLE AGE UKE

MAE GERI

㉗

⑰

⑱

㉖

㉓

㉒

⑲ + ㉑

㉓

㉔

㉖

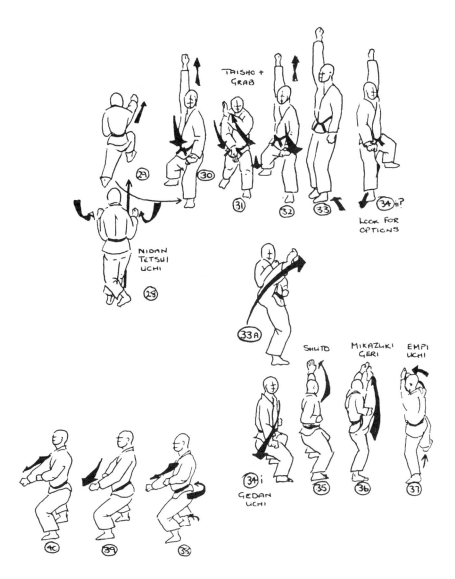

TAISHO + GRAB

29

30

31

32

33

34ii?

LOOK FOR OPTIONS

NIDAN TETSUI UCHI

29

33A

SHUTO

MIKAZUKI GERI

EMPI UCHI

34i

GEDAN UCHI

35

36

37

40

39

38

These kata are performed with hooking
AND SWEEPING THROWS, COMBINED WITH STRIKES
AND BLOCKS.
EXPLOSIVE STRIKES "PASSING THROUGH KIME" INTO
THE NEXT TECHNIQUE.

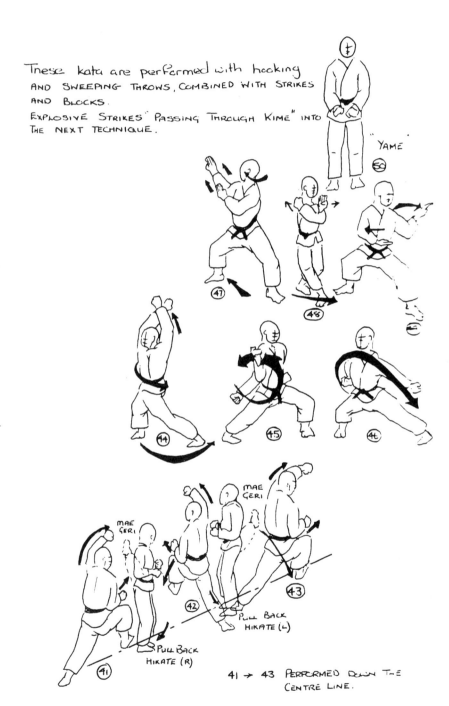

"YAME"

50

47

48

44

45

46

MAE
GERI

MAE
GERI

43

42

PULL BACK
HIKATE (L)

PULL BACK
HIKATE (R)

41

41 → 43 PERFORMED DOWN THE
CENTRE LINE.

Katas shown will take the student up to 1ˢᵗ Kyu (brown belt). The understanding of Balance and co-ordination, controlled breathing, in both defence and attack. Develop the focus of energy at the point of contact. Penetration of the technique, beyond the outer surface of the target. Performed slowly (like tai chi), to understand feeling and timing of the technique in relation to the movement, breathing and the direction of body weight. To mentally picture the opponent and know precisely your position and response to him. Every movement, twist of the wrist, transfers of weight, execution of the block, strike, kick and throw perfected. Then practiced in partner form (Bunkai) to study the practical application. The latter, then helping to develop the mental picture, ready for when the student next practices alone.

Slowly rotate the fist at the end of a punch, and on completion of that rotation, continue movement into the next and so develop fluid movement, without losing power or stability. An art form perfected, developed and made practical and effective.

Once mastered, slowly practice, introduce speed, so that several techniques are performed in a single breath. Do not sacrifice quality of the technique for speed. Speed can only be developed with time, so that the destructive force (and control) will not be lost.

A student should never let a technique turn into a flick, slap or jab. Penetration of ki energy is essential for defence, whether blocking or striking. It is this understanding that makes a block a strike, and a strike a block. Both should destroy your opponent's spirit and prevent further conflict.

Understanding this and combining it with body movement makes sparring impossible. Several attacks are prevented due to the pain, and or damage inflicted upon the aggressor on the first attempted blow.

It is this concept that prevents further development of some European students, and big powerful students who bounce around and attempt to drive home surface punches. Points may be scored, but points are not important, they are superficial, as are trophies and titles.

Perfection of yourself (not physical), mentally and technically, is the only real way to develop self-confidence, belief in your ability to overcome attacks, and so lack fear. But also lack the need to prove, need to beat, need to bully.

When you are at peace with yourself, you are ready to take the first step "Sho dan".

"The purpose of the art of Karate, is neither victory, nor defeat. But the perfecting of the character of those who practice it".

Gichin Funakoshi

CONCLUSION

It is important to say that these writings are not about my Style, my Kata or my Fighting methods. They are about developing yours, so that you can take what you know and broaden it. Expand your knowledge. Not through new movements or new techniques, but through these specific details of thought and reasoning, develop your old ones.

" Through thought and reasoning understand and improve what you already know.
Develop an open and flexible mind, so that you will be able to absorb and come to understand that which you have yet to be taught.
For none of use knows it all.
And so expand and strive to improve your art, your ability, your knowledge, your attitude, yourself".

K O'Connor